The Complete Guide to Raising Backyard Chickens

Everything you Need to Know About Chicken Keeping from A-Z to Maintain a Happy Healthy Flock and Produce Self-Sufficient Eggs and meat from Your Own Backyard

Raymond Charles

Table of Contents

Introduction

The Joy of Chicken Keeping

Welcome to *The Complete Guide to Raising Backyard Chickens*, a comprehensive manual dedicated to the joy of chicken keeping. For centuries, the practice of raising chickens in our own backyards has offered an array of rewards, from the simple pleasures of watching these feathered friends roam and scratch the earth to the more substantial gifts of fresh, delicious eggs and the satisfying experience of sustainable living.

It is important to note that raising chickens also comes with responsibilities and challenges. You need to provide proper housing, feed, and healthcare for your chickens and be prepared for unpleasant tasks like cleaning the coop, protecting them from predators, and addressing health issues when they arise. However, for many people, the benefits of raising chickens outweigh the challenges, making it a rewarding and sustainable endeavor.

If you are new to the world of chicken-keeping, you may often face a range of challenges and concerns along the way. These challenges include the complexities of setting up a coop and selecting the right equipment, dealing with issues like poor egg production, disease worries, and environmental management.

As you advance, you may grapple with sustainability goals and the complexities of expanding your flock. This guide addresses these challenges by providing practical solutions, expert advice, and valuable knowledge to help you become a confident and successful chicken keeper.

Benefits of Raising Chickens

Whether you are a small-scale backyard enthusiast or a larger-scale farmer, raising chickens can offer a variety of benefits:

- Fresh eggs: One of the most compelling reasons people raise chickens is for a steady supply of fresh eggs. Homegrown eggs often taste better and can be more nutritious than store-bought eggs.
- Meat production: Chickens can be raised for meat, providing a source of lean protein. Broilers, specifically bred for meat production, can be raised and processed for consumption.
- Pest control: Chickens are natural foragers and can help control pests in your yard or garden. They eat insects, grubs, weeds, and other garden pests, reducing the need for chemical pesticides.
- Fertilizer production: Chicken manure is rich in nutrients and makes an excellent fertilizer for gardens and crops. It can improve soil quality and enhance plant growth.

- Education and learning: Raising chickens can be a valuable educational experience for children and adults alike. It teaches responsibility as well as animal husbandry, and provides insights into the food production process.
- Low maintenance: Chickens are relatively low-maintenance animals compared to other livestock. They require shelter, food, water, and periodic health checks, but they do not demand as much care as larger animals like cows or pigs.
- Companionship: Chickens can be entertaining and even provide companionship to their owners. Many people enjoy watching their chickens and find them to be charming pets.
- Extra income: Keeping chickens for profit is a real possibility. Whether you are planning on selling eggs, meat, or chicks, there is always a demand for sustainably and ethically farmed chickens.

Sustainability and Self-Sufficiency

Keeping chickens can contribute to both sustainability and self-sufficiency in various ways:

- Raising chickens can make you more self-sufficient by providing a portion of your food supply. This can be especially important in times of economic uncertainty or disruptions in the food supply chain. It also reduces the need to rely on store-bought products that may have been produced using less sustainable or less ethical methods.
- Raising your own chickens allows you to control their diet, ensuring they eat locally sourced, organic, or non-GMO feed if you choose. This means you have more control over the quality of the eggs and meat you consume, as you know exactly how your chickens are raised and what they are fed.
- When you produce your eggs and meat locally, it reduces the

environmental impact associated with the transportation of these products over long distances.

- By keeping chickens, you can actively participate in the local food movement, which promotes sustainable agriculture, supports local farmers, and reduces the carbon footprint associated with large-scale commercial food production operations.
- Some folks raise chickens as a small-scale business, selling eggs, meat, or even chicks to neighbors and at farmer's markets to generate income.
- Chickens are excellent at recycling kitchen scraps and leftovers, which can reduce food waste in your household and contribute to a more sustainable lifestyle.
- Chicken manure is a valuable resource as a fertilizer, which can enhance the productivity of your garden or crops, reducing the need for synthetic fertilizers.
- Many chicken keepers implement sustainable practices in their coop management, such as using solar-powered coop lighting, rainwater harvesting for chicken watering, and eco-friendly coop design.

Who Should Read This Guide?

This guide is tailored to novice poultry enthusiasts who are taking their first steps into the world of chicken keeping, experienced hands seeking to deepen their knowledge and enhance their practices, and folks with a passion for self-sufficiency, sustainable living, and a connection to the land. Whether you reside in the countryside or an urban setting, you'll discover that raising backyard chickens is not only feasible but a fulfilling endeavor with numerous benefits for you and your community.

Overview of Chapters

In Chapter 1, we lay the foundation for your chicken keeping journey. We'll guide you through the initial steps, from choosing the right chicken breeds for your needs to preparing the coop. Discover the essentials of coop design, bedding, and nesting boxes, and learn how to source healthy chicks or adult birds.

Chapter 2 delves into the day-to-day aspects of chicken care. From feeding and watering your chickens to maintaining a clean and hygienic living environment, you'll gain insights into the critical tasks required to keep your flock happy and healthy. We'll also cover basic healthcare practices to prevent common chicken ailments.

Understanding your chickens' behavior is key to their well-being. In Chapter 3, we explore the intricacies of chicken behavior, helping you decipher their language and tendencies. Learn how to handle chickens safely and how their social dynamics work within the flock.

If you are interested in taking the scenic route and raising chicks from day one, Chapter 4 offers a detailed guide to chick rearing. Discover how to brood chicks, provide them with the necessary warmth and nutrition, and ensure their successful transition to outdoor living.

In an era of growing environmental awareness, Chapter 5 explores sustainable chicken keeping practices. We'll discuss eco-friendly practices, waste management, composting, and how chickens can play a role in sustainable living.

For many, the reward of fresh eggs and, potentially, homegrown meat is a significant motivation for raising chickens. Chapter 6 covers the best practices for harvesting eggs and meat, ensuring safe and ethical processing.

Chapter 7 addresses the inevitable challenges you may encounter, such as predators, pests, diseases, and behavioral issues. We provide guidance on prevention, diagnosis, and treatment to keep your flock healthy and secure.

In the final chapter, we explore the possibilities of expanding your flock or venturing into other chicken-keeping practices. Whether you're considering breeding, hatching your own eggs, or exploring other poultry varieties, Chapter 8 will help you take the next steps.

The Complete Guide to Raising Backyard Chickens will provide you with all the knowledge to confidently raise a happy and productive flock, whether you're a beginner or an experienced chicken enthusiast. Let us embark on this exciting adventure together and unlock the joys of backyard chicken keeping.

Chapter 1

Getting Started with Chickens

Choosing the Right Breed

Choosing the right breed of chicken to raise depends on your specific goals, preferences, and circumstances. Consider your personal preferences and what aspects of chicken keeping are most important to you. Whether you're drawn to a breed's egg production, its size, or specific traits, make sure these factors align with your preferences and the purpose you have in mind for your flock.

Heritage Versus Hybrid

traits, such as specific plumage colors, egg colors, or other characteristics. Decide whether you want heritage breeds or hybrid breeds. Heritage breeds may be more resilient and have unique characteristics, while hybrids are often bred for specific traits like increased egg production or meat yield.

Hybrid chickens cannot breed true because they are the result of crossing two different heritage chicken breeds. When two purebred breeds are crossbred, their offspring inherit a mix of genetic traits from both parent breeds. This means that the characteristics of the offspring will be unpredictable and will not match those of the parents.

In contrast, heritage chickens have been selectively bred for many generations to have consistent and predictable

Purpose

Determine the primary purpose for raising chickens. Are you raising them for eggs, meat, or both? Some breeds are specialized for one purpose, while others are dual-purpose.

If you're primarily interested in egg production, research the breed's egg-laying capabilities. Some breeds are prolific layers, laying upwards of 300 eggs a year, while others lay fewer eggs but may be better for meat production.

For meat production, look for breeds that are known for the quality of their meat and fast growth rate. Dual-purpose breeds are often a good choice if you want large birds for both eggs and meat.

Temperament

Chickens have different temperaments. Some are docile and friendly, while others can be more skittish or aggressive. Consider the temperament of the breed and whether it aligns with your preferences. Although much of their temperament is decided by their genetics, the environment they are raised in and their individual personalities also play a large role.

Setters and Non-Setters

Setters are broody hens that exhibit a strong maternal instinct to incubate and hatch eggs. They will sit on a clutch of eggs, maintain constant warmth, and protect the eggs until they hatch. Setters are essential for natural reproduction in chicken flocks. Some breeds are more prone to broodiness, which can be desirable if you plan to hatch your own chicks or less desirable if you want consistent egg production.

Non-setters, on the other hand, are hens that lack the instinct to brood. They are more inclined to lay eggs but do not show the behavior of sitting on the eggs to hatch chicks. Non-setting behavior is often found in commercial or egg-laying breeds that have been selectively bred for high egg production but may have diminished brooding instincts.

Noise Level and Vocalization

Chickens are not the quietest creatures around, though some breeds are quieter than others. While hens contribute their fair share to the general noise, roosters are well-known for their loud and distinctive crowing.

Roosters crow often, but usually more in the morning around dawn. A rooster's vocalizations can carry over long distances. Before getting chickens, and especially a rooster, it is important to be aware of local regulations and the proximity of neighbors who might be affected by the noise. Some chicken keepers employ soundproofing methods in the coop to mitigate the noise level, though these are often only partially effective.

Space Availability

Assess the space you have available for your chickens. Some breeds are more suited to confinement and smaller coop spaces, while others require more room to free-range.

Climate and Location

Consider your climate and location. Some chicken breeds are more cold-hardy, while others are better suited to hot climates. Choose a breed that can thrive in your local conditions. It is often a good idea to visit local poultry shows, talk to experienced chicken keepers, or consult with local agricultural extension offices for guidance on the best breeds for your specific location.

Availability

Check the availability of the breed in your area or from reputable breeders. Some breeds may be more challenging to find.

Appearance and Color

If aesthetics are important to you, consider the breed's appearance and plumage color. There is no shortage of colors, patterns, and plumage.

Maintenance

Different breeds may have varying maintenance requirements. Some breeds are hardier and more disease-resistant, while others may require more attention to health and care.

Popular Breeds for Beginners

Popular chicken breeds for beginners are typically known for their ease of care, docile temperaments, and suitability for backyard or small-scale poultry keeping.

Buff Orpington

Buff Orpingtons are dual-purpose heritage chickens that adapt well to either confinement or free range. Ideally, you would need a coop with 3–4 square feet per adult and a run with 10 square feet per adult.

This plump, broody breed lays 200—280 or more large eggs per year. Both roosters and hens are great parents and readily accept eggs that are not their own.

The adult wight is eight lb. for hens and 10 lb. for roosters. When raised for meat they reach full maturity at 22 weeks old.

They are quiet, docile birds with friendly personalities. They love attention and will often seek you out. They get along well with flockmates and with other docile chicken breeds.

Buff Orpingtons are very cold-hardy but may have trouble adapting to hot summers.

They are heavy feeders and forage very little. Hens may suffer from health issues if allowed to become overweight.

Plymouth Rock

Plymouth Rocks are large, active heritage chickens that prefer open spaces to roam and forage in. Hens weigh around seven and a half lb., and roosters weigh up to nine and a half lb. They are dual-purpose birds, laying around 200 medium to large eggs all year round, even in winter. From 18—22 weeks, hens lay eggs their entire lives, although egg production will start to slow down after three years.

Plymouth Rock is a docile breed that enjoys attention and is unlikely to fight with flockmates. They are not broody chickens but are great mothers.

There are seven recognized color varieties of Plymouth Rocks, the Barred Rock being the most iconic of the variations.

Plymouth Rocks are independent birds that require little maintenance. These healthy chickens are very cold-hardy; however, roosters' combs are prone to frostbite. Both hens and roosters can tolerate hot summers. However, they will require plenty of shade and water in extreme heat.

Rhode Island Red

The Rhode Island Red is one of the most popular heritage breeds. Roosters typically weigh around eight and a half lb., and hens weigh six and a half lb. These chickens are dual-purpose. However, they are more often kept for egg-laying, as hens can lay from 150—300 medium to large eggs per year from 18—20 weeks old. The hens are only occasionally broody and are great mothers.

Rhode Island Reds are low-maintenance, tolerant of heat and cold, and are known for their exceptional health. They are active birds who love to roam and forage.

The hens are very curious, as well as docile and friendly to people and other chickens. However, their mild temperament varies between individuals. The roosters are often aggressive.

Rhode Island Reds are quite noisy and may not be the best choice for small urban backyards.

Easter Egger

Though not technically a breed, these chickens are hybrids of Ameraucana and mixed-breed Araucana chickens. The hens weigh around four lb, and roosters weigh around five lb.

One of their most desirable traits is the color of their eggs, which can be light pink, blue, white, brown, or speckled and olive-colored. Each hen produces only one shade of egg during her lifetime and can lay 200—280 eggs per year. Hens do not often go broody.

These hardy birds have no specific health problems and are very tolerant of both hot and cold climates.

Easter Eggers are low-maintenance and readily forage when allowed to roam. They are friendly to people and flockmates, curious, and quiet birds. They may get picked on by more aggressive breeds.

Leghorn

Leghorns are very active heritage chickens and need plenty of space to roam and search for food. They are a smaller breed, with hens weighing five to six lb. and roosters weighing seven and a half to eight lb.

Leghorns are egg layers that lay 250—300 medium to large eggs per year. They are not broody and lay eggs all year round.

You may need to cover the top of their run as Leghorns like flying and perching high up.

Leghorns are independent birds that shy away from people. They can be a noisy bunch, which may be problematic in an urban environment.

These chickens tolerate hot and cold climates and generally have few health problems.

Red Star

Like the Easter Egger, the Red Star is a hybrid, dual-purpose chicken. The most frequently crossed breeds to produce Red Stars are Rhode Island Reds and White Plymouth Rock.

Red Star hens weigh around six lb., and roosters weigh eight lb. Hens start laying eggs at 22 weeks old, producing 300—360 large eggs all year round.

Red Stars are hardy birds that tolerate both cold and hot climates.

They are friendly toward people but may be more aggressive toward flock mates.

They can be noisy, and fly often, preferring to perch up high, which may be problematic in an urban environment.

Understanding Breed Characteristics

Size

Chicken breeds come in various sizes. Almost all breeds have bantam counterparts, which are typically one to two lb., to large breeds like Jersey Giants, which can weigh an astonishing 11—15 lb.

Plumage Color

Plumage colors vary widely among chicken breeds. Common colors include white, black, red, brown, buff, and various shades of gray. Some breeds have distinctive patterns, such as barred, laced, or speckled.

Comb Type

Chickens have different types of combs on their heads. The most common type is the single comb, but there are also rose combs, pea combs, and more. The comb type can vary in size and shape between breeds. It has functional roles, including regulating body temperature and displaying vitality to potential mates. It is also a good indicator of your chicken's health.

Skin Color

Chicken skin color varies between breeds. Some have yellow skin, while others have white skin. The color of the skin can also affect the color of the meat, with yellow-skinned chickens producing yellow-tinged meat.

Number of Toes

Chickens typically have four toes on each foot. Three toes face forward, and one faces backward. Some chicken breeds have five toes, such as the Sultan, Houden, and Dorking breeds.

Amount of Feathering

Feathering can vary from lightly feathered to heavily feathered. Some breeds, like the Silkie, have exceptionally fluffy plumage, while others, like the Naked Neck, have no feathers on their necks. The amount of feathering can impact the breed's cold-hardiness and appearance.

Egg Color

Egg colors can range from white to brown to blue or green. The specific egg color is determined by the breed and genetics. For example, Leghorns typically lay white eggs, while Rhode Island Reds lay brown eggs, and Easter Eggers lay many different colored eggs.

Place of Origin

Chickens were domesticated from wild junglefowl in Southeast Asia over 8,000 years ago. Since then, they have been bred into a wide variety of breeds with distinct characteristics. Different breeds originated in various regions worldwide, including Europe, Asia, and the Americas. Each breed often carries the name of its place of origin or development.

Preparing Your Space

Coop Selection and Setup

Selecting and setting up a chicken coop are some of the first steps in raising chickens. The coop provides shelter, security, and comfort for your birds. Three of the most common coop types are:

- Traditional coops: Standalone structures with walls and a roof, often on a raised platform. They can be small or large, depending on your flock size.
- Mobile coops: Structures have wheels or skids that allow them to be moved to different areas of your yard. They are ideal for rotational grazing and pest control.
- A-frame coops: Compact and easy-to-build structures. They have a triangular roof and are suitable for smaller flocks.

Nesting Boxes

Nesting boxes are essential components of a chicken coop, providing a designated area for hens to lay their eggs. They encourage hens to lay eggs in a convenient location, which makes it easier for you to collect eggs without searching for hidden nests. Nesting boxes help protect eggs from dirt, feces, and damage, ensuring that they remain clean and intact until you retrieve them. They can also serve as safe, private spaces for broody hens, allowing them to focus on hatching and caring for chicks.

Nesting Box Design

- Nesting boxes should be appropriately sized, typically around 12x12x12 inches, but larger boxes are more comfortable for the hens. Fill the boxes with a suitable bedding material such as straw, hay, pine shavings, or soft nesting pads.
- Place nesting boxes in a quiet, dimly lit, and private section of the coop to make hens feel secure while laying. Avoid nesting boxes in high-traffic areas.
- Provide one nesting box for every three to four hens to prevent overcrowding. Hens may squabble over boxes if there are too few, leading to broken eggs or eggs laid outside of their nesting boxes. When in doubt, add another nesting box. Use dividers or curtains to encourage single-hen use if your hens crowd despite having enough boxes.
- Build nesting boxes from easy-to-clean materials such as plywood, plastic, or metal. Ensure they are free of sharp edges or splinters to prevent injury to yourself and your flock.
- Nesting boxes should have sloped roofs and overhangs to prevent hens from perching on top or scratching bedding out.

Maintenance

Perform routine cleaning of the nesting boxes to remove soiled bedding, feces, or broken eggs to maintain cleanliness. A clean environment encourages hens to lay and helps keep their eggs clean.

Tips on Using Nesting Boxes

- If hens lay eggs outside the boxes, gently place the eggs inside the boxes to encourage them to use the designated area.
- Establish a daily routine for collecting eggs, so they do not accumulate and tempt hens to peck or break them.
- Some chicken keepers use curtains or dividers to give hens added privacy while they lay eggs.
- Ensure that the nesting boxes are predator-proof to protect both your hens and their eggs. Having nesting boxes above ground level is a good start; however, some breeds prefer lower or ground-level options.

Roosting Bars

Roosting bars are horizontal perches where chickens sleep and rest at night. Chickens start roosting overnight once they reach eight to ten weeks old. They prefer to sleep on a roost, as it allows them to feel secure and out of reach of potential ground predators. It improves hygiene and keeps your birds clean by raising them above the coop floor, which can be littered with droppings and debris. Properly positioned bars also ensure better ventilation throughout the coop.

Roosting bars should be positioned higher than nesting boxes and lower than any ventilation openings, where it is typically warmer and offers chickens better insulation during cold weather. Most chickens prefer to roost 2–4 feet off the ground, but the height may vary depending on the breed. Some heavy breeds might need lower roosts to prevent leg strain.

Roosting bars are more than just a place for chickens to sleep; they contribute to their well-being and overall health. Providing comfortable, well-maintained roosting bars in your chicken coop ensures that your flock enjoys restful nights and maintains a strong sense of security.

Roosting Bar Design

- Roosting bars should be wide enough for chickens to perch comfortably without crowding each other. A width of 8 inches is typically suitable, but larger breeds may need wider bars.
- Rounded or flat bars are the most comfortable for chickens to grip. Avoid square or sharp-edged bars, which can lead to discomfort and injuries.
- Common materials for roosting bars include wood, PVC pipes, metal, or even tree branches. Wood is the most popular choice because it provides a natural surface for chickens to grip, and it does not conduct heat or cold as much as metal might.
- Provide adequate spacing between roosts, typically 1–2 feet apart, to prevent crowding and pecking.

Maintenance

- Regularly clean roosting bars to remove droppings, feathers, and dirt. Clean bars promote hygiene and prevent the buildup of parasites.
- Inspect and replace roosting bars when they become damaged or show signs of wear. Rotate or switch bars occasionally to minimize wear and tear on a specific area.

Tips on Using Roosting Bars

- If you have chicks in your flock, ensure that roosting bars are accessible for them. Provide a lower, easily accessible bar for young chicks to practice roosting. Chicks can start learning to roost from as young as four weeks old.

- Position roosting bars away from walls to prevent predators from reaching in. Install barriers like netting or wire mesh to keep predators at bay.
- In larger flocks, provide multiple roosting bars to reduce crowding and prevent lower-ranking birds from getting pushed out of the prime roosting spots.
- Place materials like straw or wood shavings beneath the roosting bars to absorb droppings.

Security

Ensure the coop is predator-proof. Use secure locks and latches on doors, windows, and vents. Install hardware cloth or welded wire mesh with small openings to reinforce larger openings.

Access

Make sure you have easy access to the coop for feeding, egg collection, and cleaning. Consider human-sized doors and removable panels for cleaning.

Basic Coop Design

A basic chicken coop design should provide a safe, comfortable, and functional space for your chickens to feed, drink, sleep, rest, nest, and take shelter in. A well-designed basic chicken coop should cater to all these needs while also being easy for you to manage and maintain. Customizing the design to suit the specific needs of your flock and your local climate is essential for successful chicken keeping.

A basic coop must include the following elements:

- Designated areas for nesting, roosting, and feeding. These areas should be well-organized to prevent overcrowding and disputes among the flock.
- Proper ventilation to regulate temperature and moisture levels. Install vents or windows with wire mesh to provide fresh air while keeping predators out.
- Insulation to help maintain a comfortable temperature inside and to keep chickens warm in winter and cool in summer. Proper insulation is especially important if you live in an area with extreme weather conditions.
- Horizontal roosting bars for chickens to perch on at night.
- Nesting boxes where hens can lay eggs.
- Doors for easy access for cleaning, egg collection, and feeding. Consider adding a human-sized door to make maintenance easier and a smaller chicken-sized door to allow your birds in and out.
- Easy cleaning with features like removable droppings trays, hinged roofs, or doors that allow access to all areas.
- Predator-proofing. Use strong materials, secure latches and locks, and wire mesh on windows and vents to keep out predators.
- Windows or light fixtures to provide chickens with natural or artificial light. This is especially necessary for their well-being and egg

production.

- A floor which is made of a material like plywood or concrete, as they are easy to clean and disinfect. Cover the floor with suitable material or a liner.

- A layer of bedding material inside the coop to keep the environment clean, insulate against the cold and offer a comfortable surface for the chickens.

- Connect the coop to an outdoor run, allowing chickens access to fresh air, sunlight, and space for foraging and exercise.

- Private spaces with dividers for hens to lay eggs and feel secure.

- Feeders and waterers in the coop to provide access to food and clean water. Keep them elevated to prevent contamination.

- Items for mental stimulation, such as treat balls, dust baths, mirrors, and objects to peck at. Boredom can lead to negative behaviors.

Safety Considerations

Safety considerations must be taken to ensure your own well-being and the welfare of your chickens within their living space. Regular monitoring and maintenance are key to preventing accidents and injuries and ensuring safety over time.

Keeping Yourself Safe

- Ensure that the coop and run have adequate lighting, especially if you need to access them during early morning or late evening hours.

- Use non-slip flooring materials both inside and outside the coop to prevent accidents caused by wet or slippery surfaces.

- Wear appropriate safety gear such as gloves and eye protection when cleaning the coop, or performing maintenance tasks to reduce the risk of injuries.

- If you have electrical installations in or around the coop, like lighting and heating, ensure they are properly installed to prevent electrical hazards. Protect electrical cords from being pecked at by curious chickens.

- Keep flammable materials away from heating devices and ensure proper wiring practices to minimize the risk of electrical fires.

- Design coop access points and pathways to accommodate your mobility and make it easy to reach nesting boxes, feeders, and waterers.

Keeping Your Chickens Safe

- Prioritize predator-proofing the coop and run to keep your chickens safe from nighttime threats. Use hardware cloth or welded wire mesh with small openings to reinforce large openings like vents and windows. Burying part of the fencing of stationary coops helps to deter burrowing predators. Common predators include raccoons, foxes, weasels, snakes, and birds of prey.

- Ensure proper ventilation to prevent respiratory issues in chickens. Adequate airflow will also help reduce moisture buildup, which can lead to health problems.

- Design roosting bars or perches to prevent chickens from crowding together. This can reduce the risk of aggressive behaviors and injuries from pecking.

- Ensure that nesting boxes are comfortable and free from sharp edges that can injure the chickens.

- Use suitable bedding material in the coop to absorb moisture, provide insulation, and prevent foot injuries. Avoid slippery or hard surfaces.

- Maintain a clean coop and run to minimize the risk of disease transmission and footpad injuries. Regularly remove droppings and replace soiled bedding.

- Protect chickens from extreme weather conditions by providing shade in hot weather and insulation or heating in cold weather.
- Ensure that feeders and waterers are secured to prevent spills and contamination, reducing the risk of bacterial infections.
- Regularly inspect the coop and run for hazards, such as exposed wires, sharp objects, or loose hardware. Remove or repair any potential dangers promptly.

Adequate Space and Ventilation

Adequate space and ventilation are crucial components of a healthy and comfortable living environment for chickens. Proper space allocation and ventilation help prevent potentially dangerous conditions for your chickens, such as overcrowding, moisture buildup, and extreme temperatures.

Adequate Space

- Ensure that the coop provides enough space for chickens to roost comfortably at night and lay eggs in nesting boxes. This will reduce stress, aggression, and the spread of diseases. The general guideline is to allow 2 square feet of coop space per chicken for bantams and smaller breeds and 4 square feet for larger breeds. If your chickens will spend extended periods indoors, plan for a little more space.

- In addition to the coop, chickens require an outdoor run area for exercise, foraging, and dust-bathing. Plan for 8–10 square feet of outdoor run space per chicken to ensure they have sufficient room to roam. More active breeds like Leghorns and Plymouth Rocks require larger runs.

- Overcrowding can cause your chickens to stress and make them aggressive, as well as increase the risk of diseases. Providing enough space reduces these risks and keeps your flock healthy and peaceful.

- Separate spaces with different purposes, such as nesting boxes, roosts, and feeding areas. This separation helps prevent crowding and competition during feeding and egg-laying.

- If you're using a portable coop, ensure that it is moved regularly to provide fresh forage and prevent overgrazing in a confined space.

Ventilation

- Proper ventilation allows fresh air to enter the coop while expelling stale, moist air. Natural ventilation can be achieved through windows, vents, and openings in the coop.

- Adequate ventilation helps reduce moisture buildup, which can lead to respiratory issues and frostbite in cold climates. Moisture buildup can occur from chicken respiration, droppings, and water spillage.

- Maintain ventilation year-round, even in cold weather. Cold drafts should be avoided, but there should still be a consistent exchange of air to remove excess humidity.

- Place vents or windows higher up on the coop to allow warm, moist air to rise and escape, while cooler, fresh air enters from lower openings.

- Design the coop to allow for cross ventilation, where air can flow through the coop from one side to the other. This promotes air exchange, prevents stagnation, and reduces ammonia odors to maintain healthy air quality.
- Consider roof vents or ridge vents to allow warm air to escape from the top of the coop. Ensure that these vents can be opened or closed as needed.
- In hot weather, proper ventilation helps control temperature and humidity, preventing heat stress in chickens.
- During winter, provide ventilation without exposing chickens to cold drafts. Use baffles or adjustable openings to regulate airflow and prevent the coop from getting too cold.

Sourcing Your Chickens

Buying Chicks Versus Adult Hens

Buying Chicks

Raising chicks can be a rewarding learning experience, especially for beginners. You get to experience how they grow and develop. Raising chicks allows you to bond with them and socialize them from an early age, leading to friendlier, more docile chickens. Starting with chicks also allows you to monitor their health from an early age, making it easier to detect and address any issues.

Chicks are generally less expensive to purchase than adult hens, although you will need to invest in brooding equipment such as heat lamps, brooder boxes, and feeders. They require more time and attention during their early stages, including maintaining proper temperature and providing specialized chick feed.

It takes several months for chicks to mature and start laying eggs, so you'll need to be patient if you're primarily interested in egg production.

Buying Adult Hens

With adult hens, you can see their physical characteristics, including size, plumage, and temperament, before buying them. However, the best advantage to buying adult hens is that you skip the time-consuming chick-rearing phase and can focus on maintaining the coop and run. Adults require less hands-on care than chicks, as they do not need to be monitored for temperature or specialized feeding.

Adult hens will start laying eggs right away, providing you with a quicker return on your investment if egg production is your primary goal.

There are a few drawbacks to buying adult chickens:

- Adult hens are generally more expensive to purchase upfront compared to chicks. However, you save on the cost of brooding equipment.
- Your choices may be limited to the hens available for sale in your area, and you may not have the same variety of breeds to choose from as you would with chicks.
- You may not know their complete history, including any past health issues, vaccinations, or living conditions.
- Adult hens may be less inclined to bond with you than chicks raised from a young age. However, this can vary depending on the individual hen's temperament.

Local Hatcheries and Breeders

Sourcing your chickens from local hatcheries and breeders is a popular and practical approach for many backyard poultry keepers. This method offers several advantages, such as supporting local businesses, obtaining healthy and well-adapted birds, and having the opportunity to personally inspect your chickens before purchase.

Advantages

- Local hatcheries and breeders often have valuable knowledge about the specific needs of chickens in your region, including climate considerations and breed suitability.
- You have the opportunity to establish a good rapport with the sellers, ask questions about the birds' history and care, and ensure that you're comfortable with the conditions in which the chickens were raised. This approach allows you to make informed decisions and obtain healthy, well-suited birds for your backyard flock.
- You can inspect the chickens in person, assessing their health, plumage, and behavior before making a purchase. This minimizes the risk of introducing diseased birds into your flock.
- Local sources may have a better selection of breeds and varieties suited to your climate and preferences. They may also offer rare or heritage breeds that are hard to find elsewhere.
- Purchasing from local hatcheries and breeders supports small-scale agriculture and local businesses, contributing to the sustainability of your community.
- Transporting chickens over long distances can be stressful for the birds. Sourcing locally minimizes travel time, reducing stress and the risk of injury or disease transmission.
- Local breeders and hatchery owners may provide you with guidance and support for your chicken-keeping endeavor, including information on care, nutrition, and housing.

Considerations

- The availability of specific breeds or varieties may be limited to what local sources have on hand. If you're looking for rare or uncommon breeds, you may need to consider a broader search.
- Local sources may charge higher prices compared to large commercial hatcheries. However, the quality and individualized care of locally sourced chickens can justify the cost.
- While local sources may reduce the risk of disease introduction, it is still important to practice good biosecurity by quarantining new chickens before introducing them to your existing flock.
- Before purchasing from a local source, research their reputation and visit their facilities if possible. Verify that they follow best practices for chicken health and care.
- Ensure that your local zoning and poultry-keeping regulations allow you to keep chickens and purchase from local sources.
- If you need to transport the chickens from the source to your home, ensure you have appropriate transportation containers and minimize travel time to reduce stress.
- Check if the chickens you intend to purchase are compatible with your existing flock in terms of breed, size, and temperament.

Quarantine Procedures

Quarantine procedures are essential when introducing new chickens to your existing flock or bringing chickens to their new home, as it helps prevent the spread of diseases and parasites that can threaten the health of your entire flock.

To ensure a successful quarantine, implement the following steps:

1. Isolate new chickens: Set up a separate, isolated area for the new

chickens. This should be a completely separate coop and run if possible. If you do not have extra housing, use a partition within your existing coop and run.

2. Health assessment: Examine the new chickens for any visible signs of illness or parasites. Look for symptoms such as sneezing, coughing, runny eyes or noses, diarrhea, lethargy, or unusual behavior. Also, check for external parasites like mites or lice, as well as signs of feather loss or rough plumage.

3. Quarantine period: Quarantine new chickens for a minimum of two to three weeks, although longer periods may be necessary if you suspect any health issues. During this time, monitor the new birds closely for signs of illness or parasites.

4. Separate supplies: Use separate equipment, such as feeders, waterers, and cleaning tools, for the quarantined chickens to avoid cross-contamination with your existing flock.

5. Biosecurity measures: Wash your hands and change your clothes and footwear after handling the quarantined chickens. Maintaining good biosecurity practices minimizes the risk of disease transmission within your flock.

6. Veterinary examination: If possible, consult with a veterinarian to conduct a thorough health examination of the new chickens and do testing for common poultry diseases. This can help detect underlying health issues that may not be immediately apparent.

7. Deworming and treatment: Administer appropriate deworming and treatment for external parasites as recommended by a veterinarian or based on your observations.

8. Observation and record-keeping: Keep a record of any symptoms, treatments, or observations during the quarantine period. This information can be helpful in diagnosing and managing any potential health issues.

9. Introduction: Only introduce the new chickens to your existing flock after the quarantine period is complete, and you are confident that they are healthy. Monitor the interactions between the new and existing chickens closely to ensure there is no bullying or aggression.

10. Ongoing monitoring: Continue to monitor the health of all chickens in your flock regularly. Be vigilant for any signs of illness or changes in behavior.

Chapter 2

Daily Care and Maintenance

Feeding Your Flock

Types of Chicken Feed

Choosing the right type of feed for your chickens depends on their age, purpose (egg-laying or meat production), and dietary requirements. Providing a balanced diet ensures that your chickens receive the necessary nutrients for their growth and health. Always follow the feeding recommendations on the feed label and consult a poultry expert or veterinarian if you have specific concerns about your flock's nutrition. The primary types of chicken feed are:

Starter Feed

- Purpose: Designed for newly hatched chicks six to eight weeks of age.
- Composition: Contains high levels of protein, typically 20—24%, to support rapid growth and development. Contains essential vitamins and minerals.
- Texture: Fine crumbles to make it easy for chicks to eat.
- Use: Ideal for chicks until they are old enough to transition to a grower or layer feed.

Grower Feed

- Purpose: Intended for juvenile chickens from six to eight weeks old to around 16—20 weeks.
- Composition: Contains less than 1.25% calcium and less than 15—16% protein. Contains essential nutrients to support growth.
- Texture: Pellets or crumbles.
- Use: Provides balanced nutrition for young chickens during the growth phase to aid development.

Layer Feed

- Purpose: Designed for laying hens after they reach maturity and start laying eggs, typically around 16—20 weeks and sometimes up to 32 weeks old.
- Composition: Contains 16—18% calcium to support eggshell production, and 16% protein.
- Texture: Pellets, crumbles, or mash.
- Use: Provides the essential nutrients needed for egg production. It can be fed to both meat and egg-laying breeds.

Broiler Feed

- Purpose: Formulated for chickens raised for meat production.
- Composition: Contains high levels of protein, typically around 20—23%, to promote rapid muscle development and growth.
- Texture: Pellets or crumbles.
- Use: Provides the necessary nutrients for fast weight gain and meat production in broiler chickens.

Scratch Grains

- Purpose: Used as a supplemental treat rather than a complete feed.
- Composition: Typically includes whole or cracked grains like corn, barley, wheat, and oats.
- Use: Given to chickens in addition to their regular feed to provide variety and entertainment, and to encourage natural foraging instincts. It should not be the primary source of nutrition and must not exceed 10% of your chickens' diet.

All-Purpose Poultry Feed

- Purpose: Offers a balanced diet suitable for a mixed flock of chickens, including layers and non-layers.
- Composition: Typically has moderate protein levels and can be fed to chickens of various ages.
- Texture: Usually available in pellets or crumbles.
- Use: Convenient for mixed flocks where individualized feeding is not practical.

Organic Feed

- Purpose: Similar to standard feeds but made with organic ingredients and produced following organic farming standards.
- Composition: Varies by type (starter, grower, layer, etc.) and brand.
- Texture: Available in various forms, including pellets, crumbles, and mash.
- Use: For those who prefer to feed their chickens organic, non-GMO, and chemical-free feed.

Medicated Feed

- Purpose: Contains medications like amprolium to prevent or treat coccidiosis, a common poultry disease.
- Composition: Contains standard feed ingredients with added medication.
- Use: Administered as a preventive measure or as directed by a veterinarian when coccidiosis is a concern.
- Type of Feed Medicated: Most starter feeds are medicated, but growth and layer feeds are typically not. Withdrawal dates on these feeds indicate when to stop medicating if there is a risk of the medicine contaminating the eggs or meat.

Fermented Feed

- Purpose: Fermented feed is a method of processing chicken feed to improve its digestibility and nutritional value. The primary purpose is to enhance the overall health and well-being of chickens by increasing nutrient availability and supporting their digestive systems.
- Composition: Typically consists of regular chicken feed, such as grains, seeds, and pellets, mixed with water. The mixture undergoes a fermentation process that involves the action of beneficial bacteria

and yeast. This process can also include the addition of other ingredients like probiotics and organic matter.

- Texture: Fermented feed has a softer and slightly moist texture compared to dry feed. The fermentation process breaks down complex carbohydrates, making the nutrients more accessible to chickens. It may resemble a wet, porridge-like consistency.
- Use: Offered to chickens as a part of their daily diet. It can replace or supplement dry feed, depending on the preference and feeding practices of the poultry keeper.
- Benefits: It can improve digestibility, making nutrients more available for absorption. The beneficial microorganisms in the fermentation process can promote gut health, enhance the immune system, and reduce the risk of digestive issues. Additionally, fermented feed can lead to increased egg production, improved eggshell quality, and healthier feathers. It can also be a way to reduce feed waste and increase the utilization of feed resources.

Harmful Foods

Chickens are generally good at foraging and finding their own food, but there are several foods that can be harmful to them should they find and ingest it. Provide chickens with a balanced diet and refrain from feeding them anything that could be toxic or detrimental to their health, such as the following:

- Avocado: Avocado contains a toxin called persin, which is harmful to chickens and can lead to digestive issues, heart problems, and even death.
- Chocolate and coffee: Both of these contain theobromine and caffeine, which are toxic to chickens and can cause heart and nervous system problems if ingested.

- Onions and garlic: These vegetables contain compounds that can damage a chicken's red blood cells and lead to anemia. Feeding onions or garlic in large quantities is especially dangerous.

- Moldy or spoiled food: Moldy or spoiled food can contain harmful mycotoxins that can make chickens sick. Always ensure that their food is fresh and free from mold.

- Raw beans: Raw beans contain a compound called lectin that is toxic to chickens. Cooking beans thoroughly can break down the lectin and make them safe to eat.

- Green potatoes and tomatoes: The green parts of potatoes and unripe green tomatoes contain solanine, a toxic substance that can be harmful to chickens if ingested in large quantities.

- Rhubarb leaves: Rhubarb leaves contain oxalic acid, which can be toxic to chickens and lead to kidney damage and other health issues.

- Junk food: Feeding chickens junk food like candy, chips, or sugary snacks can lead to obesity, diabetes, and other health problems. Stick to a balanced chicken feed for their primary nutrition.

- Salty foods: Excessive salt intake can lead to dehydration and diarrhea in chickens. Avoid feeding them salty foods like chips and pretzels.

- Citrus: While small amounts of citrus fruits like oranges and lemons are generally safe, feeding chickens large quantities can lead to digestive upset due to their acidity, as well as reduced egg laying.

- Dairy: Chickens have difficulty digesting dairy products like milk and cheese because their bodies don't make as much lactase as mammals do. Dairy can lead to digestive issues and diarrhea.

- Meat scraps: While chickens are omnivores and can eat a little cooked meat, avoid feeding them meat scraps from your kitchen, especially if it is raw or seasoned.

- Excessive bread: Bread is not toxic to chickens, but it is nutritionally poor and can fill them up without providing essential nutrients.

- High-sugar foods: Foods high in sugar, such as candy, pastries, and desserts, should be avoided as they can lead to health issues.

Feeding Schedule

Establishing a consistent feeding schedule for your chickens will ensure they receive the appropriate amount of nutrition and maintain good health. The feeding schedule can vary depending on the breed, age, and purpose of your chickens (layers, meat birds, or mixed flock):

- Birth to eight weeks old (Chicks): Chicks should have access to a starter feed at all times to support their rapid growth.

- Eight to sixteen weeks old (Growers): Continue to offer grower feed to juvenile chickens at all times.

- Sixteen weeks old and upward (Layers or Meat Birds): Provide layers with access to layer feed at all times. Provide meat birds with access to broiler feed at all times.

Additional Feeding Considerations

- Treats and supplements: In addition to their primary feed, you can offer chickens a variety of treats like vegetables, fruits, and grains in moderation. These should complement their diet, not replace it.

- Grit: Provide chickens with access to poultry grit, which helps them digest food by grinding it in their gizzard. Grit is especially important for birds that forage.

Feeding Times and Routine

- Chickens are naturally inclined to forage throughout the day. They will eat small amounts of food multiple times during daylight hours.

- Provide feed in a clean and dry feeder that prevents waste and keeps the feed free from contamination.

- Monitor the feed level in the feeder regularly and refill it as needed to ensure chickens always have access to food.

Adjustments for Seasonal Changes

- In cold weather, chickens may need more calories to stay warm. Consider providing supplemental grains or increasing their feed intake.

- In hot weather, chickens may eat less. Ensure they have adequate access to fresh water to stay hydrated.

Supplements and Treats

Supplements

Supplements for chickens can be beneficial to address specific nutritional needs, support overall health, or enhance egg production. It is important to note that supplements should be used judiciously and in consultation with a veterinarian or poultry expert. An excessively supplemented diet can lead to imbalances and health issues. It is best to provide a well-balanced and nutritionally complete chicken feed as the primary source of nutrients and use supplements only when necessary or recommended by a professional.

Some common supplements for chickens are:

- Calcium supplements: These are essential for laying hens to support strong eggshell formation. Crushed oyster shells or limestone can be provided in a separate container for hens to consume as needed.
- Shell grit: Grit supplements are small, hard particles that help chickens digest food in their gizzards. Insoluble grit, such as small stones or granite, aids in grinding down food. Soluble grit, like crushed eggshells, provides calcium.
- Probiotics: Probiotic supplements contain beneficial bacteria that support gut health in chickens. They can improve digestion and nutrient absorption and enhance the immune system.
- Vitamins: Vitamin supplements can be administered to address specific deficiencies, but they are not usually necessary if chickens have a balanced diet. Vitamin D and B-complex supplements are sometimes used.
- Electrolytes: Electrolyte supplements can be added to water during periods of heat stress, illness, or other stressful situations to help chickens stay hydrated and maintain electrolyte balance.
- Molting supplements: These supplements provide extra protein, amino acids, and nutrients to support chickens during the molting process when they shed old feathers and grow new ones.
- Parasite control: Natural supplements like diatomaceous earth, which is a fine powder made from the fossilized remains of diatoms, can help control external parasites like mites and lice.
- Omega-3 fatty acids: Supplements like flaxseed or fish oil can be added to the diet to increase omega-3 fatty acids in eggs, improving their nutritional content.
- Amino acid supplements: These can be used to enhance the protein content in the diet, particularly for meat chickens.

Treats

In addition to their primary feed, you can offer chickens a variety of treats in moderation. These should complement their diet but not replace it:

- Fruits: Chickens relish fruits like apples, pears, bananas, and berries. Be sure to remove any seeds, pits, or cores that may be harmful.
- Vegetables: Offer vegetables such as carrots, broccoli, peas, and leafy greens. They provide essential nutrients and can be a healthy addition to their diet.
- Mealworms: Dried mealworms are a protein-rich treat that chickens find irresistible. They are great for a protein boost.
- Cracked corn: Cracked corn is a common treat for chickens. It is energy-rich and can be used as a training reward.
- Scratch grains: Scratch grains are a mixture of different grains like corn, wheat, and oats. They are a favorite treat for chickens and can be scattered on the ground for them to scratch and peck.
- Yogurt: Plain, unflavored Greek yogurt is a good source of probiotics and can promote gut health in chickens. It contains less lactose than regular yogurt. However, it should still be given in moderation.
- Bread: Stale bread can be given as an occasional treat, but it should not be the primary source of calories.
- Pasta: Cooked pasta without added salt or seasoning can be an enjoyable treat for chickens.
- Leftovers: Chickens can enjoy kitchen scraps like rice, oatmeal, or scrambled eggs in moderation. Avoid feeding them anything spoiled or moldy.
- Fresh herbs: Chickens like fresh herbs like parsley, basil, and cilantro. These can also have some health benefits.
- Pumpkin: Chickens often relish pumpkin, and it can be a seasonal treat. The seeds are also edible and nutritious.

Watering and Hydration

Providing Clean Water

Chickens require access to fresh water at all times, especially in warmer climates and during hot weather.

- Use clean water containers, such as waterers or troughs, that are specifically designed for poultry. Ensure that the containers are free from dirt, debris, and algae.
- Elevate waterers slightly off the ground to prevent contamination by droppings, bedding, or mud. This also helps keep the water cleaner.
- Clean and sanitize water containers regularly, ideally once or twice a week. Use a mild detergent, rinse thoroughly, and ensure there are no soap residues left behind.
- Replace the water daily or as needed to ensure it remains fresh. Chickens can be picky about water quality, and they may reduce their intake if the water is not clean.
- Automatic drinkers and cups connected to a water supply can save a lot of time and effort. You will still need to check the water flow daily, and multiple times in hot weather.
- Use spill-proof or drip-proof waterers and check for any leakage to minimize water wastage and prevent the coop or run from becoming wet and messy.
- Place water containers in a shaded area to prevent overheating in hot weather. In cold weather, provide some form of protection from cold winds or a heating device to prevent water from freezing and becoming inaccessible to your chickens. Automatic drinkers may freeze and break if left running in frigid temperatures.

Winter Water Solutions

- Heated waterers: Invest in heated waterers designed for poultry. These units have heating elements that prevent water from freezing in cold temperatures. Be sure to follow safety instructions when using electrical devices in or around the coop.

- Insulation: Insulate the water container or provide insulation around the waterer to help retain heat and delay freezing. You can use foam insulation sleeves or wrap the waterer with insulating materials.

- Frequent checking: Check the water multiple times a day in freezing weather. Break up any ice that forms, and add warm water to the container to melt any ice that has already formed.

- Heating pads: Some poultry keepers use heating pads designed for outdoor use to keep water from freezing. These can be placed under or around the water container.

- Use sunlight: Place waterers in sunny areas during the day to take advantage of solar heating. This can help prevent freezing during daylight hours.

- Preventative measures: Prevent freezing by adding electrolytes or apple cider vinegar to the water, which lowers the freezing point slightly. However, use these additives sparingly and ensure they are appropriate for chickens.

- Collect snow: In areas with frequent snowfall, you can collect fresh snow and bring it to the chickens. Snow often contains enough moisture to meet their hydration needs.

- Provide warm grains: Offering warm, cooked grains like oatmeal or warm water mixed with feed can help provide hydration and warmth in cold weather.

- Use large containers: Larger water bowls take longer to freeze, which reduces the frequency at which you'll need to check it.

- Keep the water surface moving: Placing floating objects in the water container delays freezing by rippling the surface. The wind may help by blowing them around and causing more ripples.

Coop Cleaning and Maintenance

Regular Cleaning Routine

Cleaning the chicken coop helps to maintain a healthy and comfortable living environment for your chickens. A clean coop helps prevent the buildup of waste, odors, pests, and diseases. To simplify planning for these tasks, organize them by how frequently they should be done:

Daily Tasks

- Collect eggs daily to prevent them from getting dirty or cracked.
- Empty, rinse, and refill water containers to provide fresh, clean water for your chickens.
- While not a cleaning task, daily checks of your chickens for signs of illness or injury are essential to catch problems early.

Weekly Tasks

- Remove any soiled bedding material from nesting boxes and replace it with clean straw or shavings. This keeps eggs clean and discourages broody hens from sitting on dirty nests.

- Use a shovel or rake to scrape up accumulated droppings from the coop floor and run. Dispose of the droppings in a compost pile or dispose of them according to local regulations.

- Replace the bedding material on the coop floor. Clean, dry bedding helps absorb moisture and droppings, reducing odors and the risk of disease.

- Inspect the coop for any leaks or areas of dampness that could lead to mold or bacterial growth. Address leaks promptly.

- Check vents and openings for blockages or debris that might hinder airflow. Clean or replace ventilation components as needed.

Monthly Tasks

- Thoroughly clean the coop. Remove all bedding, nest box material, and droppings. Sweep and scrape all surfaces to remove dust, debris, and cobwebs.

- After cleaning, disinfect surfaces with a poultry-safe disinfectant to kill any remaining pathogens. Allow the coop to air out before adding fresh bedding.

Seasonal Tasks

- Spring and fall are ideal times for deep cleaning. Empty the coop completely, scrub all surfaces, and replace bedding. Check for any repairs needed before winter.

- Examine roosts for signs of wear or damage. Replace them if necessary to maintain a secure place for chickens to sleep.

As Needed

- Address Pest Issues: Regularly check for signs of pests like mites, lice, or rodents. Implement pest control measures if needed, such as adding diatomaceous earth, setting traps, or using pest-specific treatments.

- Regularly inspect the coop for any needed repairs, such as loose boards, broken windows, or damaged hardware. Fix any issues promptly to ensure the coop remains secure.

Tips for Safe Cleaning

- Wear appropriate protective gear, including gloves and a dust mask, when cleaning to reduce exposure to dust and allergens.
- Avoid using harsh chemicals for cleaning, as these can be harmful to chickens. Use poultry-safe disinfectants or natural cleaning solutions like vinegar and water.
- Ensure proper ventilation while cleaning to prevent exposure to dust and fumes.

Preventing Common Coop Issues

Regular observation and a proactive approach to coop care can prevent many common issues and provide a safe and healthy environment for your chickens. Keep the following in mind when performing routine tasks:

- Perform routine cleaning and maintenance tasks to keep the coop in good condition. This includes cleaning bedding, removing droppings, and repairing any damaged or rotted wood promptly.
- Ensure proper ventilation to prevent moisture buildup, which can lead to respiratory issues and mold growth. Adequate ventilation also helps regulate temperature in both hot and cold weather.
- Implement effective pest control measures to keep mites, lice, rodents, and other pests at bay. Regularly inspect the coop and use

poultry-safe pest deterrents or traps as needed.

- Maintain secure fencing to keep predators out. Reinforce coop windows, doors, and latches to prevent access. Install hardware cloth over openings to keep out small predators.
- Keep water containers clean and free of debris to prevent contamination and disease transmission. Provide fresh water daily.
- Practice good biosecurity by quarantining new chickens before introducing them to your flock. This helps prevent the spread of diseases.
- Provide a balanced and appropriate diet for your chickens based on their age and purpose. Avoid overfeeding or underfeeding to maintain optimal health.
- Conduct regular health checks on your chickens. Look for signs of illness, injury, or stress. Early detection and treatment can prevent outbreaks and fatalities.
- Install hardware cloth or dig a barrier around the coop to prevent digging predators like raccoons or foxes from gaining access.
- Consider using deterrents such as motion-activated lights, noise devices, or guardian animals like dogs or geese to deter predators.
- Prepare the coop for seasonal changes. Ensure it is well-insulated and weatherproof in winter, and provide shade and ventilation in hot weather.
- Avoid overcrowding the coop, as it can lead to stress, aggression, and the spread of disease. Provide sufficient space for your flock.
- Quarantine new chickens, ducks, or other poultry additions for at least two weeks before introducing them to your established flock.
- Maintain cleanliness in the outdoor run area. Remove any stagnant water, spoiled feed, or debris that can attract pests and lead to unsanitary conditions.
- Stay informed about common chicken health issues and diseases.

Knowing the signs and symptoms can help you detect problems early.

- If you notice signs of illness or unusual behavior in your chickens, consult a poultry veterinarian for proper diagnosis and treatment.

Health and Wellness

Signs of a Healthy Chicken

As you learn to recognize the signs of a healthy chicken, you will become more adept at spotting when your chickens are not feeling their best. Any unusual behavior or signs should be investigated as soon as possible, not only for the individual chicken's sake but for the welfare of your entire flock. Healthy chickens are more productive and have a better quality of life. The following are signs of good health:

- Active and alert: Healthy chickens are active and alert, moving around the coop or run with purpose. They are curious and responsive to their surroundings and the presence of their keeper.
- Bright eyes: Healthy chickens have bright, clear eyes with no discharge or swelling. Their eyes should be alert and responsive to movement.
- Clean vent area: The vent area or cloaca should be clean and free from feces or signs of diarrhea.
- Normal droppings: Healthy chickens produce well-formed droppings that are typically brown or green. Watery or extremely loose droppings can indicate a health issue.
- Healthy plumage: Feathers should be clean, shiny, and free from bald patches, lice, or mites.
- Good appetite: Healthy chickens have a strong appetite and eagerly consume their feed. They actively forage for insects, plants, and other

food sources in the coop or run; however, some breeds are more active foragers than others.

- Well-hydrated: A healthy chicken should have access to fresh water at all times and drink regularly. Dehydration can lead to sunken eyes and lethargy.
- Smooth movement: Chickens should move with coordinated and smooth motions, without limping, stumbling, or showing signs of lameness.
- Clear breathing: Chickens should breathe quietly and without audible wheezing or coughing. Nostrils should be clear and free from discharge.
- Normal body condition: A healthy chicken should have a well-rounded body with an appropriate amount of fat covering the breastbone. - Emaciation or obesity can be signs of health issues.
- Active dust bathing: Chickens engage in dust bathing to clean their feathers and skin. Healthy chickens will actively participate in this behavior.
- Social interaction: Healthy chickens interact well with their flock mates and exhibit normal social behaviors, such as grooming and preening each other.
- Normal egg production: For laying hens, consistent egg production is a sign of good health. However, egg production can decrease during molting or in response to environmental stress or age.
- Normal egg quality: Healthy hens lay eggs with strong shells and good yolk consistency. Thin-shelled eggs or eggs with irregularities can be a sign of nutritional deficiencies.
- Normal vocalizations: Chickens communicate with each other and their keepers through vocalizations. Healthy chickens produce normal clucks, squawks, and chirps.
- No Signs of aggression or bullying: Chickens should not exhibit

excessive aggression or bullying within the flock. Minor squabbles are normal, but severe or prolonged aggression can indicate stress or health issues.

It is important to remember that chickens can hide signs of illness, so regular observation is crucial. Familiarize yourself with the baseline behavior and appearance of your flock so that you can quickly identify deviations from normalcy. If you suspect a chicken is unwell, it is best to consult a poultry veterinarian for a proper diagnosis and treatment. Early intervention can often prevent more serious health issues from developing.

Molting

Molting is a natural process in which chickens shed and regrow their feathers.

- Purpose: Molting is essential for maintaining the health and vitality of chickens. Over time, feathers become worn and damaged. Molting allows the growth of fresh, new feathers, ensuring better insulation and protection from the elements.
- Frequency: Chickens typically undergo a major molt once a year, usually in the late summer or fall. This coincides with the decrease in daylight hours and helps them conserve energy for feather regrowth. Molting is temporary, but if it is excessive or accompanied by other signs of illness like lethargy or stress, it may be a sign of an underlying illness.
- Duration: Molting can last several weeks, during which chickens may appear scruffy and lose some of their plumage.
- Effects on egg production: During molting, hens redirect their nutritional resources toward feather regrowth rather than egg production. Molting is a physically demanding process, and egg production often decreases or stops for the duration of the molt.
- Care and nutrition: Providing a well-balanced diet rich in protein and

essential nutrients is crucial during molting. Offering supplemental protein sources like mealworms, black oil sunflower seeds, or high-quality poultry feed can support feather regrowth.

- Environmental considerations: To help chickens stay warm and comfortable during molting, ensure they have access to shelter and protection from extreme weather conditions.
- Behavioral changes: Chickens may become more sensitive or timid during molting, as they may experience discomfort and increased vulnerability due to their reduced plumage.

Common Chicken Ailments

Chickens are susceptible to various health issues and ailments, some of which are more common than others. It is important for you to be aware of these common chicken ailments, their symptoms, and potential treatments.

Respiratory Infections

- Common symptoms: Sneezing, coughing, nasal discharge, labored breathing, and wheezing.

- Common causes: Bacterial or viral infections, poor ventilation, or overcrowding.

- Treatment: Isolate affected birds, improve coop ventilation, provide clean bedding, and consult a veterinarian for antibiotics if necessary.

Coccidiosis

- Common symptoms: Diarrhea, blood in feces, lethargy, hunched posture, reduced appetite, and weight loss.

- Common causes: Protozoan parasites (Eimeria species).

- Treatment: Administer coccidiostats or anticoccidial medications, improve hygiene, and consider prevention through vaccination.

External Parasites (Mites and Lice)

- Common symptoms: Feather loss, skin irritation, restlessness, anemia, and reduced egg production.
- Common causes: Infestation by external parasites like mites and lice.
- Treatment: Dust chickens with poultry-friendly dust or spray with appropriate treatments. Thoroughly clean and treat the coop.

Worm Infestations (Internal Parasites)

- Common symptoms: Weight loss, diarrhea, reduced egg production, poor growth, pale comb, and wattles.
- Common causes: Infestation with internal parasites like roundworms, tapeworms, or gapeworms.
- Treatment: Replace water sources with garlic-infused water or administer dewormers based on fecal tests and veterinarian recommendations. Practice good pasture management to reduce reinfection.

Egg-Laying Problems

- Common symptoms: Egg abnormalities such as soft-shelled eggs or shell-less eggs, egg binding, or prolapsed vents (protrusion of the cloaca). The hen might display a fluffed appearance, straining, lethargy, and distress.
- Common causes: Nutritional deficiencies, stress, genetics, or underlying health issues.
- Treatment: Address underlying causes, provide a balanced diet,

including calcium supplements, and give them warm baths. In severe cases, the egg must be removed manually by a veterinarian.

Sour Crop

- Common symptoms: Swollen, squishy crop, bad breath, reduced appetite, or lethargy.
- Common causes: Fermentation and blockage in the crop due to overeating or eating indigestible materials.
- Treatment: Empty the crop, provide water with electrolytes, and monitor food intake. Avoid overfeeding and ensure a balanced diet.

Pasty Butt (Vent Gleet)

- Common symptoms: Accumulation of feces around the vent area, leading to blockage and discomfort.
- Common causes: Poor sanitation, stress, or fungal infections.
- Treatment: Clean the affected area gently with warm water, apply antifungal ointment, and improve coop hygiene.

Fowl Pox

- Common symptoms: Warty lesions or scabs on the skin and inside the mouth, reduced appetite, and weight loss.
- Common causes: Viral infection (Fowlpox virus).
- Treatment: Provide supportive care, keep affected birds isolated, and consult a veterinarian for severe cases.

Botulism

- Common symptoms: Paralysis, inability to eat or drink, drooping wings, and general weakness.

- Common causes: Consumption of contaminated water or feed.

- Treatment: Supportive care and isolation. Prevention is key to proper sanitation and water management.

Marek's Disease

- Common symptoms: Paralysis, weakness, tumors, and eye changes.
- Common causes: A highly contagious viral disease.
- Treatment: Vaccination is the best prevention. There is no cure once chickens are infected.

Prevention through good management practices, proper nutrition, and regular health checks is often the best way to avoid common chicken ailments.

Consulting with a veterinarian or poultry specialist can help diagnose and treat health issues promptly to minimize their impact on your flock.

Veterinary Care

While chickens are generally hardy birds, they can still suffer from illnesses and health issues that require professional medical attention. Early detection and treatment of health issues are essential to maintaining a healthy flock. Regular communication with your poultry veterinarian and a proactive approach to healthcare is key to preventing and addressing chicken health problems.

Find a Poultry Veterinarian

Look for a veterinarian with experience in poultry medicine. Not all veterinarians specialize in poultry, so it is important to find one who is knowledgeable about chickens. Do this before you get your chickens so you can be ready in the event of an emergency.

Regular Health Checks

Schedule regular health checks for your flock. Annual check-ups can help detect and address health issues early, preventing the spread of diseases within the flock.

Sick Bird Examination

If you notice a chicken that appears sick, isolated, or behaving abnormally, consult your veterinarian. Provide a detailed description of the bird's symptoms, including changes in behavior, appetite, and appearance.

Diagnostic Testing

Your veterinarian may recommend diagnostic tests such as fecal examinations, blood tests, and cultures to identify the cause of illnesses or infections.

Vaccinations

Some diseases, like Marek's disease and Newcastle disease, can be prevented through vaccination. Consult your veterinarian to develop a vaccination schedule for your flock.

Parasite Control

Your veterinarian can provide guidance on controlling internal and external parasites like worms, mites, and lice. Fecal tests may be needed to determine the appropriate deworming regimen.

Nutritional Guidance

Veterinarians can offer advice on providing a balanced diet for your chickens. They can also help identify and address nutritional deficiencies or imbalances.

Wound Care and Minor Surgery

In cases of injuries or minor surgical procedures like wound suturing, your veterinarian can provide the necessary treatment.

Post-Mortem Examination

If you experience unexplained deaths within your flock, your veterinarian may perform post-mortem examinations to determine the cause and prevent further losses.

Medication and Treatment Plans

Veterinarians can prescribe medications and treatment plans tailored to the specific needs of your chickens. Follow the recommended treatment regimen closely.

Biosecurity and Disease Prevention

Your veterinarian can offer guidance on biosecurity measures to prevent disease introduction and transmission. This includes quarantine procedures for new chickens.

End-of-Life Care

If you have aging chickens or chickens with incurable illnesses, your veterinarian can advise you and help you make humane end-of-life decisions.

Health Education

Veterinarians can provide you with valuable knowledge about chicken health, disease prevention, and management practices.

Chapter 3

Understanding Chicken Behavior

Chicken Social Structure

The Pecking Order

Chickens are social birds that have a structured and hierarchical social order within their flock. Understanding the social structure of chickens can help you manage your flocks and promote harmonious interactions among the birds. While chickens have their own system of hierarchy, you can create an environment that minimizes conflicts and ensures the well-being of all members of the flock.

Pecking Order (Dominance Hierarchy)

Chickens establish a pecking order, which is a ranking system that determines each bird's social status within the flock. It is established and maintained through various behaviors, including pecking, posturing, and vocalizations. Dominant birds occupy higher positions in the hierarchy, while submissive birds are lower in rank.

Dominant Versus Submissive Behavior

- Dominant chickens display behaviors such as pecking, chest bumping, and wing flapping to assert their authority.

- Submissive chickens exhibit behaviors like crouching, avoidance, and allowing dominant birds to eat first. They often show deference to dominant birds by offering their backs or necks for pecking.

Benefits of the Pecking Order

The pecking order helps maintain order and reduces aggression within the flock. It establishes a clear hierarchy, reducing the likelihood of violent confrontations. Chickens prefer a stable social structure, as it provides a sense of security and predictability.

Establishment of the Pecking Order

Chickens establish their pecking order early in life, with chicks as young as a few weeks old beginning to assert dominance, but in time, the pecking order can change as chickens grow and mature, or when new birds are introduced to the flock. Introducing new chickens can disrupt the existing pecking order, leading to temporary aggression and squabbles as the birds establish a new hierarchy.

Benefits of Understanding the Pecking Order

Understanding the social structure of chickens can help you identify and address issues like bullying, over-mating by roosters, and the need for multiple feeding and watering stations. Chickens at the lower end of the pecking order may require extra care to ensure they are not being bullied and have access to food and water.

Providing Adequate Space

To reduce conflicts and overcrowding, it is important to provide sufficient space in the coop and run, as overcrowding may lead to increased aggression.

Monitoring for Aggressive Behavior

- Keep an eye on your flock for signs of excessive aggression, injury, or stress. If a chicken is being excessively bullied, it may need to be separated from the flock temporarily.

General Behavior of Chickens

- Foraging: Chickens actively forage for food, often scratching at the ground to uncover insects, seeds, and other edible items. They alert the entire flock when they discover food sources.
- Dust Bathing: Chickens engage in dust bathing as a way to keep themselves clean and free from parasites. They scratch and fluff dust or soil onto their feathers, then shake it out, creating a cleaning process that helps protect their skin and plumage.
- Sunbathing: Chickens often sunbathe to warm themselves, especially in cooler weather. They spread their wings and bask in the sun to absorb heat, which helps regulate their body temperature.
- Exploration: Chickens are naturally curious creatures. They explore their surroundings, pecking and scratching at objects and ground

cover. This exploration is both a means of finding food and a way to interact with their environment.

- Alertness: Chickens have a strong sense of vigilance and will react to perceived threats by sounding alarms, such as loud clucking and seeking shelter. Their alertness helps protect the flock from potential predators.
- Resting and roosting: Chickens prefer to roost at night, seeking higher ground or perches to rest and sleep. This behavior helps protect them from ground predators.

Roosters

- Crowing: The crowing of a rooster is perhaps their most iconic behavior. They typically crow in the early morning to announce the beginning of a new day and to establish their presence within the flock. Crowing can also be triggered by other environmental factors or perceived threats.
- Territorial and protective: Roosters tend to be protective of their territory and the hens in their flock. They will often alert the flock to potential dangers, such as predators, by making specific calls or by displaying aggressive behavior toward perceived threats.
- Establishing hierarchy: In a flock of chickens, including hens and other roosters, a pecking order is established. Roosters typically occupy the

top of the pecking order. Dominant roosters will assert their authority through physical displays and sometimes confrontations.

- Mating behavior: Roosters court hens through displays that include strutting, puffing up their feathers, and making distinctive clucking sounds. Roosters mount and mate with hens as part of the reproductive process.
- Social interactions: Roosters have complex social interactions within the flock. They may exhibit protective behavior toward specific hens or form close bonds with particular individuals.
- Aggression: Some roosters can be aggressive, especially if they perceive a threat to their territory or hens. Aggressive behavior may include lunging, pecking, or even spurring during confrontations.
- Environmental adaptation: Rooster behavior can be influenced by environmental factors, such as temperature and daylight length. They may become less active during hot weather or adjust their crowing patterns as the days get shorter in the winter.

Note that while roosters can exhibit protective and sometimes aggressive behaviors, individual temperaments can vary based on breed, handling, and socialization. Careful management and prompt addressing of problem behaviors can help ensure that all your chickens are harmonious and productive.

Hens

- Dominant hens: Hens have their own pecking order within the flock. Dominant hens may have preferred access to nesting boxes and feeding areas.

- Nesting: Hens exhibit nesting behavior when they are ready to lay eggs. They seek out private and sheltered spots to build nests and safely lay their eggs.

- Brooding and mothering: Hens exhibit maternal behavior when they are broody. They maintain the eggs' temperature and protect them from harm, often pecking at any potential threats that come too close.

- Egg laying: The primary purpose of hens in chicken keeping is to lay eggs. The timing of egg laying can vary but typically occurs in the morning hours.

Handling and Socializing

Socializing chickens not only makes them more enjoyable pets but also makes routine tasks like health checks and egg collection easier. It is important to establish trust and a positive relationship with your chickens through patient and consistent interactions.

Handling Chickens

- The best time to begin handling and socializing chickens is when they are young chicks. Frequent, gentle handling during this time helps them become more comfortable with human interaction.
- When approaching a chicken, move slowly and avoid making sudden or loud noises. This helps to reduce stress and fear in the birds.
- When picking up a chicken, use both hands to gently but firmly support its body. Hold the bird close to your body to prevent flapping and stress.

- Chickens can sense your energy and body language. Be calm and confident when handling them. Avoid showing fear or hesitation.
- Make a habit of handling your chickens regularly, even after they've grown into adults. This keeps them accustomed to human contact.
- Reward your chickens with treats or food when you handle them. This associates human interaction with positive experiences.
- Avoid chasing chickens around the coop or run, as it can cause stress and anxiety. Instead, try to coax them to come to you using treats.

Socializing Chickens

- Spend time in the coop or run, simply sitting and observing the chickens. This gets them used to your presence.
- Chickens can recognize and respond to their keeper's voice. Talk to them softly while you're in their presence.
- Hand-feeding treats like mealworms, vegetables, or grains is an excellent way to bond with your chickens. They'll quickly learn to associate you with tasty snacks.
- Chickens have their own social structure and personal space. Respect their boundaries and avoid giving them unwanted attention.
- Watch your chickens' behavior and body language. They will communicate their comfort level through actions like preening, clucking, or relaxing.
- When adding new chickens to the flock, introduce them slowly and supervise interactions to prevent bullying while they establish a pecking order.
- Try to handle and socialize all birds in the flock equally to prevent jealousy and territorial behavior.
- Providing perches for your chickens to roost on can encourage them to come closer to you. Sit near the perches while they roost to interact with them.

- Not all chickens will be equally receptive to socialization. Some may remain shy or aloof, and that is okay. Be patient and gentle with them.

Egg Production and Laying Habits

The Egg-Laying Process

1. Ovulation: The process begins in the ovaries, where the hen's reproductive system produces ova. Each ovary contains thousands of tiny ova, but only one matures during each egg-laying cycle. Hormonal signals stimulate the release of a mature ovum from the ovary.

2. Infundibulum: After ovulation, the ovum enters the infundibulum, a funnel-shaped structure at the beginning of the oviduct (the chicken's reproductive tract). In the infundibulum, the ovum can be fertilized by sperm if a rooster is present.

3. Magnum: The ovum then moves into the magnum, where it spends about three hours. During this time, the egg white is secreted, and layers of the eggshell membranes are added.

4. Isthmus: The egg then moves into the isthmus, where the inner and outer shell membranes are formed. The isthmus takes about 75 minutes to complete its work.

5. Shell gland: The egg enters the shell gland, which is also known as the uterus, where it remains for around 20 hours. During this time, calcium is deposited onto the eggshell membranes, forming the hard, protective shell.

6. Vagina: The egg passes through the vagina on its way out of the oviduct. In the last minutes of the egg-laying process, a thin layer of mucus is applied to the egg, providing some lubrication as it is laid.

7. Laying the egg: The cloaca temporarily opens to allow the egg to pass through, and then it closes again.

8. Brooding or collection: After laying, the hen may leave the nest to eat,

drink, or engage in other activities. If she is a broody hen, she may return to the nest to incubate them. For egg collection, it is important to gather eggs promptly to prevent them from becoming dirty, cracked, or incubated.

9. Egg formation cycle:
   o Chickens have a natural egg formation cycle, with most hens producing an egg approximately every 25—26 hours. The timing can vary among individual hens and is influenced by factors like age, nutrition, and daylight length.

Maximizing Egg Production

Providing a balanced diet, appropriate lighting conditions, and proper nesting areas can help support optimal egg production and encourage your hens to lay eggs consistently. Egg production can naturally fluctuate due to factors like age, weather, and seasonal changes. By implementing the following practices and paying attention to the needs of your flock, you can maximize egg production and enjoy a consistent supply of fresh eggs from your chickens.

Choose the Right Breeds

Some chicken breeds are known for their high egg production, such as Leghorns and Rhode Island Reds. Choose breeds that are bred for egg-laying if your primary goal is maximizing egg production.

Provide Proper Nutrition

A balanced diet with the right mix of nutrients is essential for egg production. Ensure your chickens have access to a commercial layer feed. Offer calcium supplements, such as shell grit or crushed eggshells, to support strong eggshell formation.

Clean Water Supply

Access to clean and fresh water at all times is essential. Dehydration can reduce egg production and quality.

Maintain Optimal Lighting

Chickens require about 14—16 hours of daylight to maintain consistent egg production. If natural daylight is insufficient, consider using supplementary artificial lighting in the coop to extend the photoperiod. Use timers to mimic a consistent daylight schedule.

Provide Comfortable Nesting Boxes

Ensure your nesting boxes are clean, comfortable, and well-ventilated. Hens prefer to lay eggs in a quiet, darkened, and private space.

Collect Eggs Promptly

Gather eggs regularly to prevent broodiness or egg-eating behaviors. Leaving eggs in the nest can encourage hens to go broody or become more susceptible to egg-eating.

Prevent Stress

Minimize stressors in the flock, as stress can disrupt egg production. Keep the coop clean, provide adequate space, and avoid overcrowding.

Address Health Issues

Keep your chickens healthy by implementing a regular health check routine. Address any signs of illness promptly, as sick chickens are less likely to lay eggs.

Prevent Parasites

External parasites like mites and lice can stress chickens and reduce egg production. Implement a parasite control program and regularly inspect your flock for signs of infestation.

Monitor Egg Production

Keep track of your chickens' egg production. If you notice a drop in production, investigate potential causes, such as disease, stress, or environmental factors.

Replace Aging Hens

As hens age, their egg production tends to decline. Consider periodically replacing older hens with younger ones to maintain optimal production levels.

Broodiness Management

If a hen goes broody, you may need to take steps to break her broodiness to encourage egg-laying.

Handling Behavioral Issues

Dealing with Aggression

Chickens can become aggressive for various reasons, including establishing a pecking order, territorial disputes, overcrowding, or external stressors. To maintain a peaceful and productive flock, you will need to manage aggression successfully. Addressing aggression in chickens may require patience and persistence. Each flock is unique, and what works for one group of chickens may not work for another.

A few steps to deal with aggression in chickens are:

- Identify the aggressors: Observe your flock to identify the specific chickens exhibiting aggressive behavior. Note the triggers and targets of aggression.
- Separate aggressive birds: If a chicken is overly aggressive, consider temporarily separating it from the flock. Isolation can help reduce aggression and give the aggressor a chance to calm down.
- Increase space and resources: Overcrowding can lead to increased aggression. Ensure your coop and run provide ample space and resources, including feeding and watering stations and nesting boxes to prevent dominant birds from monopolizing access to food and water.
- Introduce new birds gradually: When introducing new chickens to the flock, do so gradually. Use a wire mesh or transparent screen through which the chickens can see one another, but cannot interact, allowing the birds to get used to each other's presence before you fully integrate them.
- Add distractions: Boredom can lead to aggression. Provide distractions like hanging treats or pecking toys to keep chickens occupied.
- Observe rooster behavior: Roosters can be a source of aggression, especially if they are overzealous in their mating attempts. If necessary, consider rehoming or isolating aggressive roosters.
- Address stressors: Identify and address stressors in the environment, such as loud noises, predator threats, or extreme weather conditions. Reducing stress can help reduce aggression.

- Be prepared to break up fights: If you witness aggressive behavior, be prepared to intervene by clapping your hands or gently separating fighting birds. Avoid using excessive force, as this can injure the birds.
- Apply anti-peck solutions: In some cases, you may need to apply an anti-peck lotion, such as Pick-No-More, to discourage feather-pecking and cannibalism.
- Address injured birds: Treat injured birds promptly by isolating them and providing first aid. Injured birds are vulnerable to further attacks.
- Monitor for signs of illness: Aggression can sometimes be a sign of illness or discomfort. Regularly check your flock for signs of disease or injury and consult a veterinarian if needed.
- Seek professional advice: If aggression continues despite your efforts, consult with a poultry veterinarian or an experienced poultry keeper for additional guidance and strategies.
- Cull aggressive birds (as a last resort): In severe cases where aggressive behavior poses a threat to the well-being of the flock, consider culling aggressive birds as a last resort.

Nesting and Broody Hens

Nesting Behavior

- Hens have a natural instinct to lay their eggs in a safe and secluded nesting area. They will often select a preferred nesting box or spot within the coop where they feel secure.
- Hens may scratch and rearrange the bedding material in the nesting box to create a comfortable nest. Providing clean straw, shavings, or other suitable bedding material can help them in this process.
- Most hens lay their eggs in the morning hours. They may spend some

time in the nesting box before and after laying the egg, displaying behaviors like scratching and settling into the nest.

- After laying an egg, hens may "announce" their accomplishment with a vocalization known as an "egg call." This behavior can sometimes attract other hens to the nesting box.

Broody Hens

- A broody hen is one that has the instinct to incubate and hatch eggs. During broodiness, she will seek out a nest, often becoming possessive of it and sitting on eggs.
- Broody hens may become irritable, puff up their feathers, and make clucking sounds to warn other chickens to stay away from their chosen nest. They may spend extended periods sitting on eggs, sometimes even forsaking food and water.
- To prevent excessive broodiness, collect eggs daily to ensure they do not accumulate in nesting boxes.
- Not all broodiness is desirable. If you do not want your hen to hatch eggs, you can try to break her broodiness by removing her from the nest repeatedly, providing a less comfortable nest, or isolating her in a separate area.
- If you wish to allow a broody hen to hatch and raise chicks, you can provide her with a clutch of fertile eggs or purchase day-old chicks to place under her. Ensure that she has a safe and private area to brood and raise the chicks.
- Broodiness typically lasts for about three weeks, which is the incubation period for chicken eggs. After hatching or after about three weeks, a broody hen will return to normal laying and non-broody behavior.

Egg-Eating Behavior

Egg-eating behavior in chickens can be a frustrating problem, as it leads to the loss of eggs and can be difficult to stop once it becomes a habit. Understanding the causes and addressing the issue promptly is essential.

Causes of Egg-Eating

- Chickens may peck at and eat eggs that accidentally break in the nest box out of curiosity. This can sometimes lead to them developing a taste for eggs.
- A lack of certain nutrients in the chicken's diet, particularly calcium and protein, can lead to egg-eating behavior as the hens seek to supplement their diet.
- Overcrowded conditions in the coop can lead to stress and boredom, causing chickens to engage in undesirable behaviors like egg-eating.
- Nesting boxes that allow eggs to roll out of reach or that have bright lights inside can encourage egg-eating behavior.

Preventing and Addressing Egg-Eating Behavior

- Collect eggs promptly after they are laid to prevent chickens from having access to them. Frequent egg collection is one of the most effective prevention methods.
- Ensure that nesting boxes are clean, comfortable, and well-designed to minimize the risk of eggs being accidentally broken or easily accessible.
- Feed your chickens a balanced diet with adequate levels of calcium and protein. Commercial layer feed is formulated to meet their nutritional needs.
- Provide calcium supplements like oyster shells or crushed eggshells

in a separate container for hens to consume as needed.

- Avoid overcrowding in the coop and run. Ensure that each chicken has enough space to move and access to nesting boxes.

- Place ceramic or wooden eggs in the nesting boxes to discourage pecking. When a chicken tries to peck a hard object, it may lose interest in real eggs.

- If chickens are pecking at eggs due to bright lighting in the nesting area, consider using curtains or shading to create a dimmer, more private environment.

- If you identify a chicken that is consistently eating eggs, isolate it from the flock for a period. This can break the habit.

- Observe your flock to identify the main culprits involved in egg-eating behavior and focus on addressing their needs and habits.

- In severe cases where a particular chicken consistently engages in egg-eating despite efforts to stop it, you may need to consider culling the bird to prevent the behavior from spreading to others.

Chapter 4

Raising Chicks

Hatching Eggs Versus Buying Chicks

The choice between hatching eggs and buying chicks depends on your goals, resources, and preferences. Hatching eggs offers more genetic control but requires time, equipment, and patience. Buying chicks is more convenient and typically has higher survival rates, but you may have less control over genetic traits.

Hatching Eggs

Hatching is an incredible process and represents the beginning of a chick's life outside the egg. Hatching chicks is one of the most exciting experiences of keeping chickens.

1. Choose fertile eggs from healthy, disease-free chickens, preferably from a National Poultry Improvement Plan (NPIP)-flock. Select eggs of good size, shape, and quality.

2. If you need to store the eggs before incubation, you can do so for up to seven days at a cool 50—60 °F and a humidity between 70 and 80%. Higher humidity poses the risk of causing condensation to form on the egg, which may clog pores in the eggshell or contaminate it.

3. While in storage, turn the eggs daily to prevent the yolks from sticking to the shell. Keep track of which side is up by marking the egg with a pencil.

4. Set up the incubator a day in advance to make sure that it is functioning properly. Read and follow the manufacturer's instructions for your specific incubator. Ensure it is clean and properly calibrated.

5. Place the eggs in the incubator with the larger end up. Use an automatic egg turner if available.

6. Maintain a consistent temperature of around 99.5 °F and humidity of 40—50%. Adjust settings as needed based on the incubator's recommendations.

7. Turn the eggs over three to five times a day for the first 10—12 days.

8. After seven to ten days, candle the eggs using a bright light source or a candling device to check for embryo development. Remove any clear or non-developing eggs.

9. On day 18, three days before hatching, increase the humidity to around 65—70%. This is called the "lockdown" period.

10. Chicks start pipping around day 21. Do not assist chicks during hatching unless there is a compelling reason to do so. Let nature take its course.

11. Leave the newly hatched chicks in the incubator until they are dry and fluffy, then transfer them to a warm brooder with water and food.

Advantages of Hatching Eggs

- Hatching eggs allows you more control over the genetic diversity and traits of the offspring. You can choose specific breeding pairs to produce chicks with desired characteristics.
- It can be a cost-effective way to increase your flock size, especially if you already have an incubator. It eliminates the need to purchase chicks.
- It can be an educational and engaging experience, especially for families or those interested in poultry breeding.
- Starting with hatching eggs from a known and healthy source can reduce the risk of introducing diseases or parasites into your flock.

Disadvantages of Hatching Eggs

- Hatching eggs can be more challenging than buying day-old chicks. Factors such as temperature and humidity fluctuations can affect hatch rates, leading to disappointment if the eggs do not hatch successfully.
- It requires a longer time commitment, typically around 21 days, compared to purchasing day-old chicks, which are ready to start growing immediately.
- While it can be cost-effective in the long run, buying an incubator and related equipment represents an initial investment.
- You need a dedicated space for an incubator and brooder to accommodate hatched chicks.

Buying Chicks

Buying chicks is an exciting endeavor, whether you're a beginner or an experienced poultry keeper. You can visit local farm stores or hatcheries or source chicks online for a greater variety of breeds. Here are some tips on making the right choices when purchasing chicks:

1. Decide whether you want to raise chickens for egg production, meat, or both.
2. Choose a trusted and reputable source for your chicks. Options include local hatcheries, breeders, feed stores, and online sellers. Research their reputation, reviews, and quality.
3. Determine your budget for buying chicks. Prices can vary based on breed, quantity, and source. Be prepared for costs beyond the purchase, including feed, housing, and healthcare.
4. Select breeds that align with your goals—research various breeds for characteristics like egg-laying ability, temperament, and appearance.
5. Where possible, examine the chicks yourself for signs of health. They should be active, alert, and free from deformities. Look for clean, dry vent areas, bright eyes, and smooth feathers.
6. Depending on your preferences, choose between day-old chicks, pullets (female chicks nearing point-of-lay), or older chickens. Day-old chicks

require more care but allow you to raise them from a young age.

7. Set up a clean and secure brooder before bringing the chicks home. Ensure it has proper bedding, heat, food, and water.

8. Transport the chicks in a well-ventilated, secure container. Protect them from drafts and provide warmth for the journey home.

9. When you bring your chicks home, place them in the prepared brooder, and offer them food and water. Monitor their behavior and ensure they settle in comfortably.

10. Chickens grow quickly, so be prepared to transition them to a suitable coop or outdoor space as they mature.

Advantages of Buying Chicks

- Day-old chicks tend to have a higher survival rate compared to hatching eggs. They have already successfully hatched and are ready to grow.

- Buying chicks eliminates the incubation period, allowing you to focus on raising and caring for young birds right away.

- You do not need to invest in an incubator or monitor temperature and humidity as closely as you would with hatching eggs.

- Chicks are readily available from hatcheries, feed stores, local breeders, or poultry clubs, providing a wide range of breeds and varieties.

Disadvantages of Buying Chicks

- When you buy chicks, you have limited control over their genetic traits. You may not get the specific characteristics you desire.

- Chicks can experience stress during transportation, which may affect their health and overall well-being.

- Chicks from unknown sources can potentially introduce diseases into your flock. It is crucial to obtain chicks from reputable and disease-free sources.

- Although you do not need an incubator, you will still need to set up a brooder for your young chicks.

Brooder Setup and Temperature Control

Setting Up a Brooder

- Choose a suitable container: You can use a cardboard box, a plastic tub, or a dedicated brooder designed for this purpose. Ensure that it is clean and free from any harmful substances.
- Line the bottom of the brooder with suitable bedding material. Pine shavings, straw, or paper towels are common choices. The bedding should be clean, dry, and non-toxic while also providing grip for the chicks.
- Provide a heat source to maintain the appropriate temperature. A heat lamp, heat pad, or a specialized brooder heater can be used. Ensure that the heat source is secured and positioned to prevent contact with the chicks or bedding.

- Provide a feeder and a waterer suitable for chicks. Ensure that the waterer is shallow to prevent chicks from drowning. Keep food and water clean and replenish them regularly.

- Provide enough space in the brooder to allow the chicks to move around comfortably. Overcrowding can lead to stress and aggression.

- Provide a light source that mimics natural daylight for 18—20 hours each day. A red or infrared heat lamp can be used. Maintain a consistent light-dark cycle to promote healthy development and avoid disturbing sleep. Too much bright light may also lead to aggression.

- Ensure that the brooder has good ventilation to prevent the buildup of ammonia.

- Make sure the brooder is secure and protected from drafts, predators, pets, and other hazards. Set it up in a place with low foot traffic. Keep it away from direct sunlight or extreme temperature fluctuations.

- Regularly observe the chicks to check for signs of distress, illness, or discomfort. Healthy chicks are active, alert, and exhibit normal behavior.

Temperature Control

Place a thermometer at chick level to monitor the temperature. Adjust the heat source as needed to achieve the following temperature ranges:

- **Week 1:** Keep the brooder temperature at around 95 °F.
- **Week 2:** Reduce the temperature to 90 °F.
- **Week 3:** Lower the temperature to 85 °F.
- **Week 4:** Gradually decrease the temperature by 5 °F per week until it reaches the ambient room temperature.

Feeding and Caring for Chicks

Food

Begin feeding chicks with high-quality commercial chick starter feed from day one. This feed is specifically formulated to meet the nutritional requirements of growing chicks. It contains essential nutrients such as protein, vitamins, and minerals. Monitor the protein content in the starter feed. Account for local factors and seasonal changes. Local environmental conditions can affect the availability of certain feed ingredients. Be flexible in your feeding practices to adapt to these variations.

- For broiler chicks, aim for around 20—22% protein.
- For layer chicks, 18—20% protein is sufficient.
- While chick starter feed is primary, you can introduce small quantities of grains like cracked corn, oats, or barley as treats, but do not exceed 10% of their diet.
- Chicks have high energy demands, so offer food and water 24/7. They eat frequently and will self-regulate their intake.
- If chicks are raised on slippery surfaces or indoors, they may benefit from a small dish of fine grit to aid digestion and help minimize the risk of splayed legs.

Water

Provide clean, fresh water at all times. Use a shallow dish to prevent drowning. Maintain water levels and add a few shiny rocks, free from contaminants, to their water dishes for the first few days to attract chicks and encourage them to drink. This also serves the purpose of keeping the young bird's heads above water, as they may nod off and topple headfirst into the water.

Caring for Chicks

- Observe the chicks daily for signs of distress, illness, or discomfort. Healthy chicks are active, alert, and exhibit normal behavior.
- Consult a poultry expert or veterinarian for vaccination recommendations, especially if you're raising chickens in an area with common diseases. Practice biosecurity to prevent disease transmission.
- Ensure proper ventilation to prevent ammonia buildup from chick droppings. Good airflow promotes healthy respiratory development.
- Offer at least 0.5—1 square foot of space per chick to prevent crowding, which can lead to stress and aggression.
- Handle chicks gently and frequently to socialize them. Positive interactions with humans can result in friendlier adult chickens.
- Keep the brooder secure from potential threats, including rodents, pets, and small children.
- Practice biosecurity by limiting contact with other birds and animals. Quarantine new chicks and equipment to prevent disease transmission.
- Wash your hands thoroughly with soap and water after handling chicks to prevent the spread of diseases like salmonella.
- Regularly inspect chicks for signs of external parasites and manage them as needed.
- When they're ready, at around six to eight weeks of age, gradually transition the chicks to a suitable coop or outdoor enclosure.

Integrating Chicks with the Adult Flock

Integrating chicks with adult chickens is a process that requires careful planning to ensure a smooth transition for both your young chicks and your established flock and minimize stress or potential conflicts.

Before Integration

- Wait until your chicks are fully feathered and at least eight to twelve weeks old. They should be similar in size to the adult chickens.
- Quarantine them for at least two weeks to monitor their health and ensure they are free from diseases.
- Observe your adult chickens for signs of aggression, particularly any aggressive individuals. Identify any overly aggressive birds to be separated or rehomed if necessary.

Introducing Chicks

- Initially, keep the chicks in a separate enclosure that allows them to see and hear the adult chickens. Use wire mesh or fencing to allow both groups to see each other without direct contact.
- Allow them to observe each other for a week. This helps them get used to the presence of the other without physical interaction.
- Allow the chicks and adult chickens to interact under supervision. This can be during free-range time or in a supervised area within the coop or run.
- Ensure your coop and run have enough space to accommodate the entire flock comfortably. Place additional feeders and waterers to prevent competition for resources.
- Pay close attention to the body language and behavior of both groups. Occasional pecking and minor disputes are normal as they establish the pecking order.
- If curious behavior turns aggressive or a chick is consistently being targeted, remove it temporarily and reintroduce it later. A dog crate

within the coop can serve as a safe space for a chick to retreat if needed.

- Continue supervised interactions for a few weeks.
- After successful daytime interactions, allow the chicks to roost with the adult chickens at night. This is a significant step towards full integration.
- Even after integration, continue to observe their interactions. In rare cases, aggression can resurface, and further adjustments may be necessary.

Tips for Success

- Feeding your chickens together can help reduce competition and encourage cooperation.
- Ensure there is enough space for both groups to dust bathe, an essential chicken behavior.
- Offer environmental enrichment, like hanging cabbage or other treats, to keep chickens occupied and reduce boredom.
- Patience is key when integrating chicks with adult chickens. It may take several weeks for them to establish a harmonious pecking order.

Common Chick Health Issues and Solutions

Coccidiosis

Coccidiosis is a common and contagious intestinal disease caused by protozoan parasites known as coccidia. This disease primarily affects chickens and other poultry.

Coccidiosis can manifest in various forms, with symptoms that may range from mild to severe, depending on the extent of the infection.

Symptoms: Lethargy, diarrhea, blood in feces, ruffled feathers, reduced appetite, weight loss, and decreased egg production.

Solution: Vaccinate chicks as a preventative measure, or Isolate infected birds, and administer coccidiosis medication such as Amprolium. Maintain clean, dry bedding. Prevent overcrowding and stress, which may accelerate the spread of the disease.

Respiratory Infections

A respiratory infection is an illness that affects the respiratory system, including the throat, trachea, and air sacs. These infections can be caused by various pathogens, such as bacteria, viruses, or fungi.

Symptoms: Sneezing, coughing, nasal discharge, swollen and watery eyes, reduced appetite, lethargy, and labored breathing.

Solution: Isolate sick birds, provide good ventilation, and maintain proper coop hygiene. Consult a veterinarian for antibiotics if necessary. Treatment may involve antibiotics or antiviral drugs, depending on the cause of the infection. Administer medications as prescribed by the veterinarian and ensure that all affected birds receive the full course of treatment.

Worm Infestations

A worm infestation, also known as helminthiasis, refers to the presence of parasitic worms within a chicken's gastrointestinal tract. These parasites can be internal and may affect a chicken's health and productivity.

Symptoms: Weight loss, pale comb and wattles, ruffled feathers, lethargy, drop in egg production, diarrhea, and visible worms in feces or around the chicken's vent.

Solution: Treatment typically involves deworming medications prescribed by the veterinarian. These medications can come in various forms, such as oral solutions, powders, or pellets. Follow the recommended dosage and treatment schedule carefully.

If the infestation is still in the early stages it can be treated with a simple garlic infusion:

1. Crush or finely mince fresh garlic cloves. Use about one to two cloves of garlic for every four to six liters (one to one and a half gallons) of drinking water.
2. Place the minced or crushed garlic in a container and add the water to create an infusion. Garlic contains allicin, a natural compound that has anti-parasitic properties. Let the mixture sit for at least 24 hours, allowing the allicin to infuse into the water.
3. Replace the chickens' regular drinking water with garlic-infused water. Provide the garlic water as their sole source of drinking water for about 1—2 weeks.
4. Depending on the severity of the infestation or if you are using it as a preventive measure, you may choose to repeat the garlic treatment periodically.

Practice rotational grazing to break the worms' life cycle. Regular deworming, good biosecurity practices, and a clean living environment are key components of a comprehensive worm management strategy.

Marek's Disease

Marek's Disease is a highly contagious and deadly viral disease that is caused by the Marek's Disease virus. Marek's Disease can result in various clinical forms and symptoms, and it is a significant concern in commercial poultry farming.

Marek's Disease can present in three primary forms:

- Nervous form: Chickens may exhibit paralysis or weakness, especially in the legs and wings. This is known as Marek's disease, with neurological symptoms. Infected birds may have difficulty standing or walking.
- Ocular form: Symptoms may include irregularly shaped pupils and blindness. Chickens with the ocular form may have difficulty seeing and may appear disoriented.
- Visceral form: This form affects the internal organs, causing tumors to develop in various tissues, such as the liver, spleen, and lungs. Affected chickens may experience weight loss, depression, and respiratory distress.

Solution: Marek's Disease is challenging to treat, and there is no cure once chickens are infected. Therefore, the emphasis is on prevention and management. It may be necessary to cull infected birds to prevent the spread of the virus to other chickens.

Vaccination is the most effective way to prevent Marek's Disease. Chicks should be vaccinated at a young age to provide protection. Consult with a veterinarian to establish a vaccination program suitable for your flock.

Lice and Mites

Lice and mites are common external parasites that can affect chickens. Spotting these parasites early is crucial for maintaining the health and well-being of your flock.

How to spot lice and mites:

Lice are tiny, flat, wingless insects that may be pale, gray, or brown. They are often found near the base of feathers, especially around the vent, under the wings, and around the neck and head. Adult lice and their eggs (nits) are visible on the feathers or skin.

Mites are even smaller than lice and may not be easily visible to the naked eye. Common types of mites in chickens include Northern fowl mites, scaly leg mites, and red mites. They typically hide in cracks, crevices, or beneath the scales on the legs. You may see red or black mites crawling on the skin or feathers during a mite infestation.

Symptoms: Scratching, disheveled feathers and feather loss, lethargy, and skin irritation.

Solution: Infestations can be treated with dusting or spraying products designed for poultry. These products should be applied directly to the affected areas, such as the vent, under the wings, and the legs.

Clean and disinfect the coop and nesting boxes. Pay special attention to cracks and crevices where mites hide.

Some chicken keepers use food-grade diatomaceous earth in the coop and dust baths to help control parasites. Be cautious when using it around chickens, as inhaling diatomaceous earth can be harmful.

Vent Gleet

Vent gleet, also known as cloacitis, is a common condition in chickens characterized by inflammation and infection of the cloaca. It can be uncomfortable and potentially serious if left untreated.

Symptoms: Inflammation, swelling, thick yellowish discharge, and feather loss around the vent. Foul-smelling and watery droppings, and, reduced egg production, misshapen lethargy

Solution: Isolate chickens showing symptoms of vent gleet to prevent the potential spread to the rest of the flock. Maintain a clean and dry coop and nesting boxes. Ensure proper ventilation and remove wet bedding and droppings regularly.

Pay close attention to the cleanliness of the vent area. You may need to clean the affected chicken's vent gently with warm, soapy water and then rinse thoroughly. Avoid injuring the area further.

Vent gleet is often caused by a fungal infection, so treatment may involve antifungal medications prescribed by the veterinarian.

Probiotics can help restore the natural balance of gut bacteria and support the bird's overall health during and after treatment.

Sour Crop

This condition is also known as crop stasis or crop impaction. The crop becomes impacted and fails to empty properly. A healthy chicken's crop should empty overnight and become flat as the food inside passes through to the stomach. This condition can lead to discomfort and potentially serious health issues.

Symptoms: A swollen crop that feels doughy or fluid-filled, bad breath, regurgitation, difficulty swallowing, white patches in the mouth, lethargy, and diarrhea.

Solution: Isolate chickens showing symptoms. Gently massage the crop to aid digestion and withhold food for 24 hours, offering probiotics or apple cider vinegar instead. After fasting, reintroduce a soft, easily digestible diet, such as moistened pellets or oatmeal. Provide clean water with electrolytes.

In some cases, sour crop may be associated with a fungal infection. Consult with your veterinarian for guidance on using antifungal medications.

Heat Stress

Heat stress occurs when chickens are exposed to high temperatures and are unable to adequately dissipate heat. Chickens are especially susceptible to heat stress because they lack sweat glands and regulate their body temperature primarily through respiration.

Symptoms: Panting, drooping or spreading wings, lethargy, pale combs and wattles, and dehydration.

Solution: Provide shade, cool or icy water with electrolytes, and better ventilation. Wetting the ground and hanging wet towels in the coop can also help reduce temperature.

Feed chickens early in the morning or later in the evening to help reduce metabolic heat production during the warmest part of the day.

Injury or Pecking

Injury to chicks can be accidental, or the result of aggressive behaviors from other chickens called pecking.

Symptoms: Visible injuries or pecking wounds.

Solution: Isolate injured birds, clean and disinfect wounds, and use anti-pecking remedies like Blu-Kote.

Navel or Umbilical Hernia

A navel or umbilical hernia in chickens is a condition where a portion of the intestines or other abdominal organs protrudes through an opening or weakness in the abdominal wall near the navel or umbilical area. Hernias can vary in size and severity and are a concern in poultry health.

Symptoms: A visible, soft swelling or lump near the navel area that may appear red and inflamed. The size of the lump can vary. Affected chicks may be less active due to discomfort and lethargy.

Solution: Isolate affected chicks to prevent potential pecking or injury from other flock members. As hernias require surgical correction, the affected birds may require culling.

Leg and Foot Issues

Chickens can experience various leg and foot issues that can affect their mobility and overall well-being.

Bumblefoot

A bacterial infection on the bottom of a chicken's feet.

Symptoms: Swollen, scab-like lesions on the sole of the foot or pad ranging in color from reddish-pink in the early stages and brownish-black in the later stages. Affected chickens will be reluctant to put their weight on the foot and will limp or favor one leg.

Solutions: Consult a veterinarian for diagnosis and treatment, which may include surgery to remove the abscess. Maintain clean and dry bedding in the coop to prevent infection. Provide soft and dry surfaces in the coop and run.

Spraddle Leg or Splay Leg

It is often a congenital condition, but can also develop due to environmental factors during the chick's early development.

Symptoms: One or both legs splay outward, making it difficult for the chick to stand, balance, or walk. Affected chicks may lie flat on their belly.

Solution: Early intervention is critical. Apply leg splints or orthopedic bands to support and realign the legs. Monitor and adjust the splints regularly as the chick grows. Gently exercise the chick's legs by moving them into a more natural position for short periods several times a day. Provide a non-slip surface for chicks to stand on, such as a rubber mat.

Scaly Leg Mites

These are tiny parasitic mites that infest the legs and feet. They burrow under the scales on a chicken's legs, causing irritation and discomfort.

Symptoms: Scaly and raised leg scales. Crusty, whitish deposits on the legs. Affected birds may have difficulty walking and scratch or peck at their legs. Severe infestations can cause leg deformities and lameness.

Solution: Soak the legs in warm, soapy water to soften the scales, then gently remove the softened scales with a soft brush. Apply petroleum jelly or vegetable oil to suffocate the mites. Repeat treatment regularly until the issue is resolved.

Osteoporosis

A condition where the bird's bones become weak and brittle, leading to a higher risk of fractures. This condition is somewhat different from human osteoporosis but shares the characteristic of bone density loss.

Symptoms: Thin or brittle bones that can lead to fractures, bone deformities, and lameness. Laying hens may experience calcium deficiency.

Solution: Provide a nutritionally balanced diet with adequate calcium for laying hens. Ensure proper access to sunlight or artificial lighting to stimulate vitamin D synthesis.

Preventive Measures

More often than not, most of your chickens' health problems can be prevented. Early detection, proactive care, and preventative measures are key to maintaining a healthy and happy flock. Here are a few preventative measures you can take to ensure your flock's health:

- Maintain good coop hygiene with regular cleaning and disinfection.
- Provide a well-balanced diet and access to clean water.
- Quarantine new chickens.
- Avoid overcrowding.
- Monitor chicken behavior and health daily.
- Vaccinate against common diseases.
- Provide chickens with garlic-infused water.
- In cases of severe illness, consult a poultry veterinarian for professional guidance and treatment.

Chapter 5

Raising Chickens Sustainably

Chicken Manure and Composting

Chicken manure is a valuable resource for your garden, providing rich plant nutrients. However, it should be properly composted to ensure its safe and effective use. Proper composting ensures that it is safe, nutrient-rich, and beneficial for your plants while reducing waste and improving your garden's overall health.

Collecting and Storing Chicken Manure

- Clean your chicken coop regularly, removing droppings and soiled bedding.
- Add carbon-rich bedding material, like straw or wood shavings, to the coop. This helps absorb moisture and provides a carbon source for composting.
- Store collected manure in a designated container, such as a covered compost bin or tumbler, to prevent runoff and maintain a cleaner coop.

Composting Chicken Manure

1. Select a well-ventilated, sunny location for your compost pile or bin. Good air circulation helps speed up the composting process.
2. Build a pile, layering one part chicken manure with two parts carbon-rich organic materials. Aim for a balanced ratio of roughly 3:1 carbon-to-nitrogen.
3. You can also add crushed-up eggshells to the compost for added calcium.
4. Keep the pile moist but not soggy. Chicken manure is rich in nitrogen, which can make it too "hot" if it is too concentrated. Adding water or increasing the carbon ratio will help regulate the temperature.
5. Turn the compost regularly to ensure even decomposition and prevent odors. Aaerate the pile using a garden fork or compost tumbler.
6. Check the temperature of the pile. When it reaches around 130—150 °F, the compost heats up and kills pathogens and weed seeds. This phase may take several weeks.
7. After the heating phase, allow the compost to cure for several months. During this time, beneficial microbes continue breaking down the materials, making nutrients and minerals more available for plants and resulting in a rich, dark, and crumbly compost.

Using Composted Chicken Manure

- Once the compost is fully cured, it is safe to use in the garden. Spread it on vegetable beds, flower gardens, and around fruit trees.
- To avoid burning plant roots with a high concentration of compost, mix the composted chicken manure with garden soil. A ratio of about one part compost to two parts soil is a good starting point.
- Use the compost as a top dressing around existing plants to provide a slow-release source of nutrients. Work the compost into the top

inch of soil where possible.

- Incorporate the compost into the soil when planting new crops or transplants.

Tips and Precautions

- Never use fresh chicken manure directly in your garden, as it can be too potent and may harm plants. Composting is crucial to reduce its concentration, as well as to kill potential pathogens that may contaminate your soil. This is especially important in an edible garden where vegetables may come into contact with the soil.
- When handling chicken manure or working with compost, wear gloves to reduce the risk of disease transmission.
- Maintain a balance between carbon-rich and nitrogen-rich materials in your compost pile. This helps create a fertile and safe compost.
- Check with local authorities for regulations regarding composting and manure use.

Integrating Chickens into Your Garden

Integrating chickens into your garden is a wonderful way to create a harmonious and mutually beneficial ecosystem. Your chickens will thrive in a more natural environment and can help with pest control, fertilizing the soil, and reducing kitchen scraps, all while enjoying the fresh air and sunlight.

Garden Design and Preparation

- Consider the layout of your garden, including where you'll place flower or vegetable beds, planters, and paths.

- Designate specific areas for your chickens, such as feeding and watering stations, dust baths, and the chicken coop.
- Ensuring chickens have access to both sunny and shaded spots.
- Consider a raised-bed garden, as it allows your chickens easy access in between beds for pest control, while also minimizing the damage chickens can cause to your plants.
- Your chickens will eat or peck at just about anything, so install chicken-friendly fencing around the garden area to protect plants as well as keep chickens in.
- Chickens dig and may damage shallow-rooted plants or cause bare patches on lawns. Use hardware cloth for garden beds, and enclosures to prevent digging.

Selecting Chicken Breeds

Choose chicken breeds known for their docile temperament to minimize garden destruction. Buff Orpington and Plymouth Rock are docile breeds that will also adapt well to pets and children sharing the garden with them.

Coop and Run Design

- Place the chicken coop strategically within the garden area. This will provide easy access to eggs and simplify the daily care routine.
- Create a secure chicken run with ample space for exercise. You can use fencing or chicken wire to enclose the area. Provide shade, dust-bathing spots, and roosts.

Garden Protection

- Choose plants that are less susceptible to chicken foraging. Herbs, berries, and plants with tough leaves often withstand pecking better.

- Protect young fruit trees with chicken wire or plastic tree guards.
- Apply a layer of mulch to help protect the soil, roots, and plants. Chickens may scratch the mulch, but it helps protect against excessive foraging.

Integration Strategies

- Allow chickens to free-range in the garden, but do so under supervision. This helps you monitor their behavior and prevent damage to specific areas.
- Implement rotational grazing by fencing off different sections of the garden. Move chickens from one area to another periodically to prevent overgrazing that may lead to bare patches on your lawn.
- Create deep bed systems where chickens are allowed to scratch and turn compost in designated garden beds during the off-season.

Pest Control

Chickens love foraging for insects and can help control pests like slugs, cabbage worms, caterpillars, moths, beetles, grasshoppers, and grubs. Chickens dutifully pick insects off your plants and scour the soil for bugs. A single bird can effectively control pests in an area of up to 120 square feet.

Composting

- Feed chickens kitchen scraps, which they'll turn into valuable compost for your garden.
- Use the deep litter method in the coop. This involves adding fresh bedding material regularly, allowing the chickens to scratch and mix it with droppings, creating compost.

Regular Maintenance

Maintain a daily routine for feeding, watering, and collecting eggs. This keeps chickens content and makes them less likely to forage excessively, thereby keeping your plants protected.

Health and Safety

- Regularly inspect your chickens for signs of illness and provide proper healthcare.
- Be aware of toxic plants, and ensure they are not accessible to your chickens.
- Ensure that your pets are not aggressive toward your chickens and will not try to chase or catch them.

Enjoy the Benefits

- Savor fresh, organic eggs produced by your chickens.
- Notice improved soil quality in your garden due to composting and natural fertilization.
- Reduce kitchen waste by feeding scraps to your chickens.
- Reduced need for pest management around your garden.

Sustainable Feeding Practices

Sustainable feeding practices not only benefit your chickens' health but also contribute to a greener, eco-friendly lifestyle. By making thoughtful choices, you can reduce waste, save money, and promote eco-friendly practices.

Assess Nutritional Needs

Understanding your chickens' nutritional requirements is the first step towards sustainable feeding.

- Choose a feed suitable for feeding layers or meat birds, as their nutritional needs differ.
- Adjust the diet based on the stage of development, age, and activity level of your chickens.

Quality Feed Selection

Choose high-quality, well-balanced feeds to meet your chickens' nutritional needs.

- Commercial chicken feeds are formulated to provide the essential nutrients necessary for chickens to stay healthy and productive. Select feeds suitable for your chickens' intended use and stage of growth.
- Consider organic or non-GMO feeds to support sustainable agriculture practices.

Kitchen Scraps and Foraging

Supplement commercial feeds with kitchen scraps and foraging to reduce waste and enhance the diet.

- Feed chickens kitchen scraps like fruit peels, vegetable ends, and bread, but avoid giving them harmful foods like dairy, meat, and onions.
- Allow chickens to forage for insects and plants in a designated area to supplement their diet.

Garden Integration

Consider integrating chickens into your garden, where they can help control pests and fertilize the soil. Rotational grazing and deep bed systems can make this more effective.

Regulate Portions

Prevent overfeeding by giving chickens the right portion size. Overeating can lead to obesity and increased waste. Iceberg lettuce is not very nutritious and can cause diarrhea in large amounts.

Feeding Schedule

Establish a consistent feeding schedule to ensure that chickens get the nutrition they need while minimizing waste. Provide just as much feed as the chickens readily consume.

Proper Storage

Store feed in a cool, dry, and pest-proof location to prevent spoilage and waste.

Grit and Oyster Shells

Provide grit and oyster shells separately to help chickens digest their food and maintain proper calcium levels.

Water Management

Ensure clean, fresh water is always available. Use drip systems or nipple drinkers to minimize water wastage. However, these systems do not function well in the winter.

Herbs and Supplements

Introduce herbs and natural supplements into your chickens' diet for health benefits. Some plants, such as garlic, can help deter pests and parasites while improving the chickens' overall well-being.

Observe and Adjust

Monitor your chickens' health and weight regularly. Adjust their diet as needed, considering seasonal changes and any issues that may arise.

Breed Traits

Keep breed-specific traits in mind. Some breeds are excellent foragers and require less commercial feed. Conversely, choose breeds that do not readily forage if you want to minimize damage to your garden.

Egg Collection

Collect eggs promptly to ensure they remain clean and fresh, reducing waste.

Natural Pest Control

Chickens help control insect pests in your garden, reducing the need for chemical interventions.

Reduce Overpopulation

Avoid overpopulating your coop, as overcrowding can lead to resource scarcity and increased waste.

Managing Resources Responsibly

Responsible resource management minimizes your ecological footprint, reduces waste, and conserves resources. By making environmentally conscious choices, you can reduce costs and create a more eco-friendly and ethical approach to chicken keeping. Responsible resource management not only benefits your chicken operation but also contributes to a more sustainable and eco-friendly approach to raising chickens.

Water Conservation

- Install a drip irrigation or nipple drinker system to minimize water wastage.
- Collect rainwater for your chickens' drinking needs.
- Monitor water containers to prevent leaks and evaporation.

Recycling

Recycle materials used in your chicken operation, such as feed bags, packaging, and broken or used feeders.

Energy Efficiency

- Install energy-efficient lighting in the coop.
- Consider solar-powered coop lighting and heating options if possible.

Pest Management

- Implement natural pest control methods, such as allowing chickens to forage for insects and using predator-friendly strategies to protect your flock.
- Use tobacco or pennyroyal leaves and stems as bedding or incorporate them into bedding to make a natural deterrent against mites, lice, and fleas.
- Other aromatic herbs, such as sage, fennel, and oregano, are also good deterrents and contain natural oils that may combat germs. These oils easily transfer from bedding onto chicken feathers, saving you some time in treating the chickens, while also reducing the need for potentially harmful pesticides.

Eco-Friendly Coop Construction

- Build or renovate your coop using sustainable materials and eco-friendly practices. Wood is an excellent choice for construction material for coops, as it is naturally insulating, reducing the need for additional insulation and saving on the energy needed for running heating or cooling devices.
- Proper placement of adjustable vents in the coop can also help reduce the need for running heating or cooling systems.

Flock Size Management

Keep your flock at a manageable size to prevent overcrowding, which can strain resources and create waste. Raise only as many chickens as you need, and consider culling older, less productive chickens.

Record Keeping

Maintain records of resource use, expenses, and overall management to identify areas for improvement. Keeping records will also help you to budget and prepare for the future.

Eco-Friendly Gardening

Incorporating chicken manure compost into your garden reduces the need for chemical fertilizers. This is also safer for your flock, as it eliminates the risk of your chickens accidentally ingesting fertilizers as they forage in your garden.

Energy-Conserving Equipment

In addition to eco-friendly coop construction, invest in energy-efficient heating and cooling systems for extreme weather conditions.

Responsible Waste Management

Dispose of waste, such as bedding material, in an environmentally responsible manner. The best way is to add it to a compost heap and allow it to break down.

Local Sourcing

Source your chickens, feed, and supplies locally to reduce the carbon footprint associated with transportation.

Conservation Practices

Consider planting native plants around your coop to support local wildlife and promote biodiversity.

Education and Outreach

Share your responsible resource management practices with others in your community and online communities. By sharing information with the community, you increase awareness of sustainable practices and resource management, contributing to a more sustainable future for all.

Continuous Improvement

Regularly assess your resource management practices, seeking ways to improve efficiency, reduce waste, and minimize your environmental impact. As advances in resource management and sustainability are made, it is important to adapt to, experiment with, and adopt new practices.

Chapter 6

Harvesting Eggs and Meat

Egg Collection and Storage

Collecting and storing eggs properly is essential to ensure their freshness, safety, and quality. Whether you're raising chickens for personal use or for sale, follow this detailed guide for the best egg-handling practices:

Collecting Eggs

- Collect eggs at least once a day, ideally in the morning and again in the late afternoon. Frequent collection reduces the risk of eggs getting dirty or damaged.
- Wash your hands before handling eggs to avoid transferring contaminants from your hands to the eggs.
- Keep nesting boxes clean and dry to prevent soiled eggs. Replace bedding regularly.
- Hold eggs carefully to avoid cracking or damaging the delicate shells. Place them in a basket or container lined with clean, dry, and soft material like straw or paper towels.
- Check for any irregularities or defects. Cracked, dirty, or oddly shaped eggs should be set aside for immediate consumption or disposed of if necessary.

- If you have multiple laying hens and want to track egg freshness, consider marking the date of collection on each egg with a pencil. This helps you prioritize older eggs for use.

Cleaning Eggs

If an egg is lightly soiled, use a dry cloth or paper towel to gently wipe off the dirt. Do not wash eggs, as it can remove the protective cuticle and increase the risk of contamination. Once this natural barrier is removed, eggs must be dried off immediately and refrigerated.

Storing Eggs

- Store eggs at a consistent temperature of 45—50 °F. Avoid temperature fluctuations.
- Maintain humidity levels around 70—80% to prevent eggs from losing moisture, which can lead to poor egg quality.
- Store eggs in clean, sanitized egg cartons with the small end down to help maintain the air cell's position and quality.
- Practice first-in, first-out (FIFO) rotation to use the oldest eggs first and maintain freshness.
- Eggs can absorb odors, so store them away from strong-smelling foods or chemicals.
- If you're not using egg cartons, store eggs with the larger end up, as this can help preserve freshness.
- Eggs can remain good beyond the expiration date. Trust the float test and visual inspection more than the date on the egg or carton.
- The float test: To determine the freshness of an egg, place it in a bowl of water. Fresh eggs are dense and sink to the bottom, where they will lie on their side. Slightly older eggs will stand on one end, and stale eggs will float to the top.

Processing and Cooking Eggs

Processing Eggs

When cracking eggs, do so on a flat surface to prevent shell fragments from falling into the bowl or pan. Use a separate bowl to crack each egg individually before adding it to your recipe.

Egg Separation

For recipes that require only egg whites or yolks, use an egg separator or gently pass the yolk back and forth between the two halves of the broken shell.

Beating Eggs

When whisking eggs, use a fork or whisk. Beat them until the whites and yolks are well combined, and the mixture becomes slightly frothy. This is the base for many egg recipes.

Hard-Boiled Eggs

To hard-boil eggs, place them in a saucepan, cover with cold water, and bring to a boil. Simmer for nine to twelve minutes, then cool in cold water and peel. Hard-boiled eggs can be used for salads, deviled eggs, or snacks.

Soft-Boiled Eggs

Soft-boil eggs by bringing water to a boil, then gently placing the eggs in the boiling water. Cook for four to six minutes, then cool and serve with toast.

Poached Eggs

For poached eggs, bring water to a gentle simmer, add a splash of vinegar, and create a whirlpool by stirring the water. Crack the egg into the center of the whirlpool, allowing the swirling water to envelop the egg white. Poach for three to four minutes for a runny yolk or longer for a firmer yolk.

Cooking Methods

Eggs are a versatile and nutritious food that can be prepared in numerous ways.

Scrambled Eggs

Scramble eggs in a non-stick pan with butter or oil. Whisk the eggs with a pinch of salt and pepper, then cook over low heat, stirring gently until they reach your desired consistency.

Fried Eggs

For sunny-side-up eggs, cook them in a lightly oiled or buttered pan until the whites are set, and the yolks remain runny. For over-easy or over-hard eggs, flip them and cook until the yolks are as you prefer.

Omelets

Whisk eggs and pour them into a preheated, buttered non-stick pan. Add your desired fillings and cook until the edges are set. Fold the omelet in half and serve.

Baking and Casseroles

Eggs are used as a binding agent in baking and casseroles. Mix them with other ingredients to create quiches, frittatas, casseroles, and baked goods.

Egg-Based Sauces

Eggs are used in sauces like hollandaise and béarnaise. These sauces require a delicate balance of egg yolks, butter, and other flavorings.

Other Egg Dishes

- Eggs Benedict: Poached eggs served on an English muffin with Canadian bacon and hollandaise sauce.
- Quiche: A savory tart filled with a mixture of eggs, cream, cheese, and various ingredients like vegetables, meats, or seafood.
- Custard: A dessert made from eggs, sugar, and milk or cream, often flavored with vanilla or other flavorings.
- Meringue: Whipped egg whites and sugar used for topping pies or making delicate cookies.

Cooking Tips

- Cooking eggs over low heat prevents them from becoming tough. Slow cooking is especially crucial for omelets and scrambled eggs.

- Eggs are incredibly versatile. Try different cooking methods, add vegetables, meats, and cheeses for unique flavors and textures.

Raising Chickens for Meat

Raising chickens for meat, also known as broiler production, can provide you with a sustainable source of fresh, high-quality poultry. However, it requires careful planning, proper care, and attention to detail to ensure your flock is healthy for a successful harvest.

Planning and Preparation

- Determine the number of meat chickens you want to raise, your budget, and your desired processing method, whether processing at home or at a professional processing facility.
- Select a meat breed or hybrid known for its rapid growth and high meat yield. Common choices include Buff Orpington and Plymouth Rock.
- Purchase day-old meat chicks from a reputable hatchery or breeder. Ensure they're vaccinated against common diseases.

Housing and Equipment

- Create a clean, warm, and draft-free brooder with a heat source, bedding material, feeders, waterers, and proper ventilation.
- As meat chickens grow, transition them to a spacious, well-ventilated coop with appropriate temperature control.

Feeding and Nutrition

- Begin with a 20—24% protein starter feed for the first few weeks.
- Switch to an 18—20% protein grower feed when they're around three weeks old.

- Ensure a constant supply of clean, fresh water.
- Allow chickens to eat as much as they want to maximize growth.

Health and Management

- Maintain good biosecurity practices, including quarantine for new arrivals, regular cleaning of housing, and monitoring for signs of disease.

- Depending on your region and the prevalence of diseases, consider vaccination against common poultry illnesses.

- Provide supplemental feed like grit for digestion, and consider providing vitamins and electrolytes in their water.

Growth and Harvest

- Meat chickens are typically ready for processing at around eight to twelve weeks of age, depending on the breed and desired meat quality.

- You can process chickens at home or have them processed professionally. Ensure humane, sanitary, and efficient processing.

Post-Harvest Considerations

Store processed meat chickens in a refrigerator or freezer at safe temperatures—label packages with the processing date to keep track easily.

Learn and Adapt

Continue to educate yourself about poultry health, best management practices, and the ever-evolving field of poultry science.

Humane Slaughter and Processing

Trigger/Content Warning: The following section contains information about the humane slaughter and processing of chickens for meat. While we strive to provide a respectful and informative perspective, please be aware that the following content includes discussions of animal processing, euthanasia, and related topics that may be distressing to some readers. If you find such subjects distressing or triggering, we advise caution when reading this section. It's essential to prioritize your well-being and emotional comfort, and you can choose to skip this section if you believe it may be upsetting to you.

It is of the utmost importance to ensure the humane and ethical treatment of meat chickens throughout the slaughter and processing stages. Ethical treatment and responsible processing are not only essential for animal welfare but also for the quality and safety of the meat produced.

Preparation

- Gather all the necessary equipment. You'll need sharp knives, a killing cone or a killing station, a scalding tank, a chilling tank, heat and water-resistant gloves, and clean, food-grade containers for packaging.
- Thoroughly clean and sanitize all equipment, processing surfaces, and containers. Maintain good hygiene throughout the process to prevent contamination.

Pre-Slaughter Handling

- Approach chickens calmly and quietly to minimize stress. Avoid chasing or rough handling.
- Allow chickens access to water, but withhold food for at least 12 hours

before slaughter to allow the crop to empty out.

- Immediately preceding slaughter, pick the chicken up and turn it upside down while holding it by the lower legs.

Humane Slaughter

Cervical dislocation is a humane method for slaughtering meat chickens. Place the chicken head-down into the killing cone with its head coming out of the small end, restraining the bird and reducing the potential for suffering during the process. Hold the head and swiftly dislocate the neck by pulling the head downward.

Alternatively, you can sever the two arteries located below the chicken's ears. Allow the chicken to bleed out completely. The chicken should be motionless and unresponsive before proceeding.

Scalding and Feather Removal

- Dip and bob the chicken in a scalding tank set at 145—150°F for approximately 45 seconds to loosen feathers.
- Use a plucking machine or hand-pluck the feathers. Be gentle to avoid damaging the skin.

Evisceration

- Make a small incision and cut around the vent area to expose the cloaca.
- Insert your fingers between the breastbone and the organs and work your fingers around to make sure you loosen all the internal organs and leave the fat layer.
- Carefully reach your hand up into the carcass and grab hold of the esophagus.

- You should be able to pull out all the internal organs at once.
- Be careful not to rupture the digestive or reproductive organs and the gall bladder. Use a clean, sanitary evisceration table or surface.

Washing and Inspection

Rinse the carcass thoroughly to remove any remaining blood or debris. Inspect the carcass for any signs of contamination or defects.

Chilling

Immediately chill the carcass in a chilling tank or refrigeration unit below 40°F to quickly reduce its temperature. Keep the carcass at 40 °F for 24—48 hours to allow rigor to pass before freezing it.

Packaging

Once the chicken is chilled, package it in clean, food-grade containers—label packages with the date of processing.

Clean-Up

Properly clean and sanitize all equipment and surfaces used during processing.

Disposal

Dispose of offal and waste according to local regulations or guidelines. Consider using offal for other purposes if feasible.

Record Keeping

Maintain records of processing dates, methods used, and any observations for quality control and tracking.

Learn and Improve

Continuously educate yourself on best practices for humane poultry processing and stay informed about emerging standards so you can ensure that the entire process is humane, sanitary, and conducted with the utmost respect for animal welfare.

Storing and Cooking Chicken Meat

Storing and cooking chicken meat properly ensures its safety and flavor.

Storing Chicken Meat

Temperature Control

Store chicken meat in the refrigerator at a safe temperature of 40 °F or below. Keep it in the coldest part of the fridge, typically near the back, and for no more than two to three days.

Proper Packaging

Use airtight containers or resealable plastic bags to prevent cross-contamination and to maintain freshness.

Freezing

For long-term storage, you can freeze chicken meat. Seal it tightly in freezer-safe bags or containers. Label with the date for easy tracking. Raw chicken can be kept frozen for nine to twelve months.

Cooking Chicken Meat

Marinating

Marinating chicken in the refrigerator helps infuse the meat with flavor. Discard used marinades that have come into contact with raw chicken.

Cooking Temperatures

Ensure chicken reaches a safe minimum internal temperature. Use a food thermometer to verify:

- Whole chicken: 165 °F
- Chicken breasts, thighs, and wings: 165 °F
- Ground chicken: 165 °F

Stuffing

If you stuff the chicken, ensure the stuffing reaches 165 °F to eliminate any bacteria.

Resting Time

Let cooked chicken rest for a few minutes before slicing or serving. This helps redistribute juices, keeping the meat moist and flavorful.

Cooking Methods

Baking

Roasting chicken in the oven is a classic method. Use a roasting pan, add seasoning, and baste for extra flavor.

Grilling

Grill chicken for a smoky, charred taste. Marinate, brush with oil, and turn frequently to prevent drying.

Pan-Searing

Searing in a hot skillet and finishing in the oven is great for crispy skin. Use boneless, skin-on chicken breasts or thighs.

Frying

Deep-fry or shallow-fry chicken for a crispy texture. Use a well-drained, temperature-regulated fryer to prevent oil absorption.

Poaching

Poaching in simmering water or broth is excellent for chicken used in salads or sandwiches. Keep it at a low simmer to avoid overcooking.

Slow Cooking

Slow cookers or crockpots are perfect for tender, flavorful chicken dishes. Add seasonings, vegetables, and broth for a complete meal.

Sous Vide

Sous vide cooking involves sealing chicken in a vacuum bag and immersing it in a water bath at a precise temperature for a specified time. Finish with a quick sear for texture.

Safety Considerations

- Always wash hands, equipment, and surfaces thoroughly with hot, soapy water after contact with raw chicken to prevent bacterial cross-contamination.
- Use a separate, dedicated cutting board for preparing raw chicken.
- Avoid consuming raw or undercooked chicken as it poses health risks.
- Pay attention to safe food handling practices to prevent foodborne illnesses.
- Raw and cooked separation
  - Keep raw chicken separate from cooked chicken and other ready-to-eat foods. Store raw chicken on the lowest shelf to avoid any drips or spills contaminating other food.
- When defrosting frozen chicken meat, do so in the refrigerator or in cold water, in a sealed bag to prevent leakage. You can also use the defrost setting in the microwave.
- Cooked chicken must be stored in a fridge within two hours of being cooked and can be kept for three to four days.

Chapter 7

Common Challenges

Predators and Pests

Predators

Coyotes

- Identification: Medium-sized, dog-like mammals with pointed ears and a bushy tail.

- Prevention: Use sturdy fencing, electric fencing, or guardian animals like dogs to deter coyotes.

Foxes

- Identification: Small to medium-sized mammals with red fur and a white-tipped tail.
- Prevention: Secure coops with hardware cloth and consider using motion-activated lights or alarms.

Raccoons

- Identification: Small, masked mammals with dexterous paws.
- Prevention: Use strong locks on coop doors and reinforce openings with hardware cloth. Raccoons are adept at problem-solving, so you may need to use a padlock to secure your coop.

Hawks

- Identification: Birds of prey with sharp talons and keen eyesight.
- Prevention: Use overhead netting or covers to protect free-ranging chickens.

Owls

- Identification: Nocturnal birds of prey with a silent flight.
- Prevention: Provide secure shelter at night and use netting or enclosures for daytime protection.

Snakes

- Identification: Slender, elongated reptiles.

- Prevention: Install snake-proof wire mesh in coop openings and keep the coop area clear of debris. Snakes are excellent climbers and can squeeze into very small spaces.

Skunks

- Identification: Small mammals with distinctive black and white stripes.
- Prevention: Use traps or deterrents, and secure the coop against digging.

Weasels

- Identification: Small, long-bodied mammals with a vicious hunting instinct.
- Prevention: Use smaller gauge wire mesh and prevent access to nesting areas.

Pests

Mites and Lice

Tiny arachnids and insects that infest feathers and skin.

Signs of Mite and Louse Activity

- Chickens may appear restless, unable to settle comfortably, and may frequently preen themselves.
- Lice infest feathers and may cause damage to them, leading to a ragged or unkempt appearance. Affected feathers may also appear discolored.
- Chickens may peck at the areas where lice are active, trying to relieve

the itching and discomfort.

- You may be able to see lice crawling on the chickens' skin and feathers.

Prevention and Treatment

- Clean and sanitize the coop regularly, paying attention to cracks, crevices, and nesting boxes where these pests may hide.
- Provide a dust bath area for your chickens with diatomaceous earth or wood ash. Chickens will naturally dust-bathe to help control external parasites.
- Use poultry-safe treatment products like dust, sprays, or powders for external parasite control.

Fleas

Signs of Flea Activity

- The presence of fleas can be observed directly on the chickens, often on the skin or feathers. Fleas are small, fast-moving insects and may be visible as tiny dark specks.
- Chickens may exhibit signs of discomfort, including itching, scratching, and agitation. They may try to peck at the areas where fleas are biting.

Prevention and Treatment

- Regularly check for fleas, especially when chickens show signs of agitation.
- Use poultry-safe treatment products like dust, sprays, or powders for external parasite control.

Ticks

Signs of Tick Activity

- Ticks can be found attached to the skin, feathers, or wattles of the chickens. They are often visible as small, round, or oval-shaped, blood-feeding parasites.
- Chickens may become agitated and peck at the areas where ticks are attached, trying to remove them.

Prevention and Treatment

- Limit chickens' access to tick-infested areas and conduct regular tick checks.
- Use poultry-safe treatment products like dust, sprays, or powders for external parasite control.
- Remove and destroy all visible ticks

Flies

Signs of Fly Activity

- Flying insects around the coop.
- Large numbers of flies congregating around feed and water sources.
- Maggots may be present in areas with decaying organic matter, such as soiled bedding, wet feed, or manure.
- Flies leave behind dark fecal spots on coop walls and ceilings.

Prevention

Maintain clean coops, manage manure, and use fly traps or repellents.

Rodents

Rodents can transmit diseases, damage feed, and create unsanitary conditions.

Signs of Rodent Activity

- Small dark, oval-shaped droppings.
- Nests made of shredded paper, straw, feathers, or other materials in hidden corners of the coop.
- Gnaw marks on feed bags, wooden structures, wiring, and other coop equipment.
- Tracks in dusty or muddy areas.
- Missing feed and nibbled or contaminated feed.
- Rodents can sometimes chew small holes in chicken eggs to access the contents.

Prevention

Seal openings and use traps or bait stations to control infestations. Ensure traps and bait stations are out of reach of your chickens to prevent injury or poisoning.

Management and Prevention

Follow these guidelines to effectively protect your chickens from potential threats and ensure their safety and well-being while enjoying the benefits of raising a healthy and happy flock:

- Secure coop and run: Use hardware cloth or wire mesh to prevent access to predators, including burrowing animals.
- Lock coop at night: Predators are often most active after dark, so securely lock chickens in their coop at night.

- Guardian animals: Consider using livestock guardian dogs or other protective animals to deter predators.
- Electric fencing: Install electric fencing to deter larger predators like coyotes and foxes.
- Regular inspections: Regularly inspect your chickens for signs of pests or illnesses, and routinely clean and disinfect the coop.
- Lighting and noise: Use motion-activated lights or alarms to deter nocturnal predators.
- Proper feed storage: Store chicken feed in rodent-proof containers to prevent infestations.

Identifying Threats

Observe your flock regularly and stay vigilant about potential threats so you can quickly identify and address issues to maintain a healthy, thriving, and happy group of chickens. A proactive approach to identifying and addressing threats will ensure the success of your chicken keeping endeavor.

Disease and Health Threats

- Respiratory issues: Watch for symptoms like coughing, sneezing, nasal discharge, and labored breathing. Diseases like respiratory infections or Newcastle disease can affect chickens.
- Digestive problems: Diarrhea, pasty vent, or blood in droppings may indicate digestive issues or conditions like coccidiosis.
- Lethargy: Chickens that appear weak, lethargic, or reluctant to move may be suffering from a variety of health issues.
- Loss of appetite: Chickens who stop eating may be unwell or stressed. Ensure they have access to clean water and nutritious feed.
- Unusual behavior: Changes in behavior, such as isolation or aggression, can be a sign of stress or underlying health problems.

Predators and Pests

- Missing or injured birds: If you notice that chickens are missing or some have visible injuries, predators may be the likely culprits.
- Evidence of digging: Burrowing animals like foxes, skunks, or weasels can leave signs of digging around the coop or run areas.
- Feather loss or damage: Excessive feather loss or damage can be caused by lice, mites, or feather-pecking among flock members.

Environmental Threats

- Extreme weather: Sudden weather changes or severe weather conditions, such as extreme heat or cold, can stress chickens. Watch for signs of discomfort.
- Flooding: If your coop or run floods during heavy rain, it can pose a risk to your chickens. Assess drainage and provide dry areas.
- Mold or fungal growth: Moldy feed or damp bedding can lead to respiratory issues in chickens. Regularly check for signs of mold and address any growth promptly.

Egg-Laying Issues

- Egg abnormalities: Keep an eye out for irregularly shaped or soft-shelled eggs, which can indicate nutritional deficiencies, underlying diseases, or other health problems.
- Egg binding: A chicken struggling to lay an egg is a sign of egg binding, which requires immediate attention.

Behavioral Issues

- Aggression: If chickens suddenly become aggressive towards each other, it may indicate overcrowding, territorial disputes, or bullying.

- Depression: Chickens that appear sad, with drooping wings and tails, may be suffering from stress or illness.

Flock Dynamics

When introducing new chickens to an existing flock, monitor for bullying or aggressive behavior during the integration process.

Egg Production

A sudden, significant drop in egg production can indicate a health issue or stress within the flock.

Visual Inspections

Regularly inspect your chickens for any visible signs of distress, injury, or discomfort. Spend time observing their behavior and interactions.

Regular Health Checks

Establish a routine for checking the overall health of your flock. Monitor feed and water consumption, egg production, and overall vitality.

Consult with Experts

Seek guidance from poultry veterinarians, experienced chicken keepers, or local agricultural extension offices if you're unsure about the cause of a threat to your flock.

Predator-Proofing Your Coop

Assess Vulnerabilities

Start by inspecting your coop and run for any existing weaknesses or signs of past predator activity. Look for holes, gaps, or worn-out areas.

Secure the Coop

- Use heavy-duty hardware cloth or wire mesh with small openings of 1/2 inch or smaller to cover all windows, vents, and openings.
- Ensure doors and access points have secure locks, latches, and mechanisms that are predator-resistant.
- Install predator guards or barriers like sheet metal or concrete at the base of coop walls to prevent digging animals from burrowing underneath.
- Elevate the coop slightly to discourage digging animals and create a barrier.

Protect the Roof

- Cover the roof of the coop with sturdy materials such as corrugated metal or heavy-gauge wire to prevent climbing predators.
- Regularly trim overhanging tree branches that could provide access to the coop.

Reinforce Flooring

Use hardware cloth or solid wood to reinforce coop floors and prevent digging predators from entering.

Bury Hardware Cloth

If your coop has an open run area, bury hardware cloth a foot below the ground around the perimeter to deter digging animals.

Keep the Coop Clean

Remove food scraps and spilled feed from the coop daily to avoid attracting rodents and pests.

Nighttime Security

- Secure chickens in the coop at night, as most predators are nocturnal.
- Install motion-activated lights or alarms to deter nighttime threats.
- Set up motion-activated cameras near the coop to monitor and identify potential threats.
- Ensure coop doors are locked and sealed securely before dusk.

Guardian Animals

Consider using livestock guardian dogs, donkeys, or geese to help deter larger predators.

Regular Maintenance

Routinely inspect the coop and run for signs of wear and tear. Repair any damage promptly to maintain security.

Use Electric Fencing

Electric fencing can be an effective deterrent for large ground-based predators like raccoons and foxes.

Learn Local Predators

Be aware of the types of predators common in your area. Understanding their habits and preferences can help you tailor your security measures.

Remove Attractants

Avoid leaving chicken feed, scraps, or water outside overnight, as these can attract both predators and pests.

Seek Local Advice

Local poultry clubs, extension offices, and experienced chicken keepers in your area can provide valuable insights and advice on predator prevention.

Extreme Weather

Hot Summers and Heat Stress

Summer heat can be challenging for chickens, leading to heat stress or even death if not managed properly.

Understanding Heat Stress

Chickens are more sensitive to high temperatures because they lack sweat glands. Instead, they rely on panting and dissipating heat through their combs and wattles.

Signs of Heat Stress

- panting excessively

- drooping wings
- reduced activity
- reduced egg production
- dehydration
- combs and wattles appear darker or purple
- lethargy

Preventing Heat Stress

- Ensure your chickens have access to clean, fresh water at all times. Increase the number of water stations during hot weather.
- Provide shaded areas in the coop and run. Consider adding tarps, shade cloth, or natural shade from trees.
- Promote good airflow in the coop and run to reduce heat buildup. Use fans or open windows and vents. Ensure proper ventilation without drafts.
- Allow chickens to free-range during the cooler parts of the day, such as early morning and late evening.
- Offer frozen treats like ice blocks, watermelon, or frozen corn to help cool chickens down.
- Avoid feeding during the hottest part of the day, as digestion generates heat. Instead, feed during the cooler hours.
- Use reflective roofing materials to keep the coop cooler.
- Place shallow containers of cool water in the coop, allowing chickens to stand in the water if they choose.
- Reduce bedding material in the coop to prevent excess insulation and heat retention.
- On extremely hot days, you can lightly spray or mist chickens with water. Avoid soaking them, as wet feathers can disrupt temperature regulation.

Health and Hydration

- Ensure chickens have access to electrolytes in their water to replace lost nutrients due to heat stress.

- Monitor chickens for signs of illness, as they can be more vulnerable to disease when stressed by high temperatures.

Record Keeping

Maintain records of temperature, humidity, and chicken behavior during hot spells to help you identify patterns and adjust your management practices.

Early Intervention

Act quickly if you notice signs of heat stress. Isolate affected chickens in a cooler area, offer cool water, and provide a quiet, restful environment.

Seek Advice

Consult experienced chicken keepers or poultry veterinarians for region-specific advice on managing heat stress.

Cold Winters and Frostbite Prevention

Cold winters can present significant challenges for chickens. Frostbite is a common concern, but with proper care and prevention, you can help your flock thrive even in freezing temperatures.

Understanding Frostbite

Frostbite occurs when the extremities, such as combs, wattles, earlobes, and toes of the chicken, freeze due to prolonged exposure to cold temperatures. In severe cases, it can result in tissue damage or loss of extremities.

Frostbite Prevention

- Apply petroleum jelly or a commercial frostbite prevention product to combs, wattles, and the feet of chickens during extremely cold weather.
- Consider using chicken saddles to protect hens' backs from frostbite.

Coop Preparation

- Ensure your coop is well-insulated, draft-free, and waterproof. Use a sealant or cover any drafty gaps or cracks.
- Install windows or vents with adjustable covers to regulate ventilation without creating drafts.
- Elevate the coop slightly to prevent dampness and frost from affecting the floor.
- Provide wide, flat roosting bars for chickens to perch on. This allows them to cover their feet and minimize contact with the cold floor. Insulate the bars with straw or cardboard for additional warmth.
- Use deep litter bedding in the coop to provide insulation and warmth. Add fresh straw, pine shavings, or hay regularly.
- Consider using a safe heat source, such as a radiant heater, to keep the coop above freezing. Be cautious with heat lamps, as they can be fire hazards and cause injuries.
- Moisture can lead to frostbite. Ensure good coop ventilation to prevent condensation, but do not create drafts.

Hydration

Ensure chickens have access to clean, unfrozen water at all times. Use heated waterers or check water frequently to prevent freezing.

Outdoor Run

If your chickens have access to an outdoor run during the winter, provide shelter from wind and precipitation. Ensure the run is secure and protected from predators.

Dietary Adjustments

Increase the caloric intake of your chickens during the winter by offering additional grains, such as corn, in their diet. This provides extra energy for maintaining body heat.

Monitor Health

Pay attention to your chicken's health. Keep a close eye on the health of your flock. Watch for signs of illness or discomfort, and seek veterinary assistance if needed.

Egg Collection

Collect eggs regularly to prevent them from freezing and cracking.

Frostbite Treatment

- If a chicken develops frostbite, bring it indoors to a warm, dry environment. Gently soak the affected areas in warm water of around 100 °F to thaw and rehydrate the tissue. Avoid using hot water or rubbing and massaging.
- Apply an antiseptic ointment or a product recommended by a veterinarian to prevent infection.

- Keep the affected chicken in a warm, draft-free environment during the healing process.

Seek Advice

Consult experienced chicken keepers or poultry veterinarians for region-specific advice on managing cold winters and frostbite.

Legal Considerations

Local Regulations and Zoning Laws

Before you start or expand your backyard chicken operation, thoroughly research and understand your local regulations and zoning laws. Compliance is essential not only to ensure the welfare of your flock but also to maintain good neighborly relations and avoid legal issues. If in doubt, consult local authorities or legal experts to clarify any specific regulations in your area.

Zoning Regulations

Check your local zoning ordinances and land-use regulations. Some areas may have specific zoning designations that permit or restrict poultry keeping.

Property Size

Local regulations may specify the minimum property size required for keeping chickens. Ensure your property meets these requirements.

Distance Requirements

Regulations might stipulate how far chicken coops must be from property lines, neighboring homes, or public areas. Comply with these setback requirements.

Permits and Licenses

Determine whether you need a permit or license to keep chickens. This may involve an application process and fees.

Building Codes

Follow local building codes and regulations when constructing chicken coops, runs, or other structures. Ensure they meet safety and structural requirements.

Number of Chickens

Local regulations often limit the number of chickens you can keep. Be aware of any restrictions on flock size.

Health and Sanitation

Maintain a clean and sanitary coop to prevent odors and attract pests. Non-compliance with health and sanitation standards may result in penalties.

Nuisance Laws

Ensure that your chicken keeping activities do not create a nuisance, such as excessive noise, odors, or disturbances, to neighbors. Roosters can be noisier than hens, and some areas prohibit them due to noise concerns.

Check whether roosters are allowed in your locality.

HOA Rules

If you live in a neighborhood with an HOA, review their specific rules and regulations regarding poultry keeping. HOAs may have additional restrictions.

State and County Regulations

In addition to local regulations, check state and county laws, as they can also have an impact on chicken keeping.

Inspection and Compliance

Be prepared for inspections by local authorities to ensure compliance with zoning and health regulations.

Public Health Concerns

In some areas, there may be concerns about public health and the potential for disease transmission. Maintain good hygiene and follow recommended practices.

Education and Outreach

Engage with your local community and officials to educate them about responsible and safe chicken keeping. Address concerns and be a responsible neighbor.

Changes in Regulations

Keep an eye on potential changes in local regulations. Laws can be amended, and it is essential to stay informed about any updates that may affect your chicken keeping activities.

Chapter 8

Expanding Your Flock and Beyond

Breeding Chickens

Breeding chickens can be a sustainable solution to keeping your flock's population up, especially if you're raising meat birds. Successful breeding takes time, patience, and commitment. Do not be discouraged by setbacks; continuous learning is part of the process. Breeding is both a science and an art. Over time, you'll develop your expertise and become better at achieving your breeding goals. Your efforts in breeding can be immensely rewarding and educational as they allow you to work on improving a breed or creating unique traits.

Whether you're looking to produce your own chicks for meat, expanding your flock, or working on breeding specific traits, this chapter will walk you through the process step by step.

Selecting Breeding Stock

The foundation of successful chicken breeding begins with choosing the right breeding stock. Consider the following factors:

- Start with disease-free and healthy six-month-old chickens.
- Select chickens that conform to the breed's standard for size, shape, and feather patterns.
- Choose birds with good temperaments for easy handling and management.
- If you have specific goals for egg or meat production, select chickens with the appropriate qualities.

Setting Up Breeding Pens

To prevent unwanted mating and ensure the genetic purity of the offspring, set up separate breeding pens or coops. These pens should be designed to accommodate one rooster and a small number of hens, typically five to eight hens per rooster.

Record Keeping

Maintain detailed records of your breeding program. This includes tracking each bird's pedigree, hatch dates, egg production, and any notable traits or characteristics.

Mating and Egg Collection

Allow your selected rooster to mate with the chosen hens. For accurate record-keeping and to control which eggs are fertile, mark the eggs you intend to hatch with a pencil. Collect these eggs daily, as they can be sensitive to temperature fluctuations.

Incubation

- To hatch the fertilized eggs, you can choose between the natural way of using a broody hen or by artificially incubating the eggs.
- Artificial incubation provides more control and higher success rates but requires specific equipment.
- To ensure genetic purity, do not hatch eggs produced within the first 10—18 days of the hens being separated from other flocks with roosters. Hens may still produce eggs fertilized by other roosters for this duration.
- Fertilized eggs from your breeding pair can be expected as soon as 21—48 hours after successful mating.

Hatching and Rearing

Once the eggs hatch, provide a suitable brooding environment. This includes a brooder with heat lamps or broody hens to keep the chicks warm, clean bedding, and access to clean water and appropriate chick feed.

Selective Breeding

As the chicks grow, continue to evaluate their conformation, temperament, and production qualities. This is the time to identify the birds that best match your breeding goals.

Culling and Selection

Cull or separate birds that do not meet your breeding criteria. Select the best individuals for future breeding. Keep in mind that chicks will not always inherit the same characteristics from parents from different breeds, and not all chicks may not meet your standards.

Crossbreeding and Inbreeding

Understand the principles of crossbreeding and inbreeding. Crossbreeding can introduce desirable traits, while inbreeding can consolidate specific traits but may also magnify genetic issues. Research the breeds and consult seasoned breeders for advice.

Genetic Considerations

Learn about and understand basic genetic principles such as dominant and recessive traits. Understanding dominant and recessive traits helps predict the traits that can be passed from one generation to the next.

Dominant Traits

Dominant traits are characteristics or features that are expressed when at least one of the alleles, or gene variants for that trait is dominant. Organisms inherit one allele from each parent, and these alleles can be the same or different. The combination of alleles an individual carries at a particular location of the gene influences the physical expression of a trait.

If a chicken inherits even one copy of a dominant allele for a specific trait, that trait will be visible in their phenotype, or physical appearance.

Recessive Traits

Recessive traits are characteristics that are only expressed when an individual inherits a copy of the same recessive allele from each parent.

Recessive traits are only visible in the phenotype when an individual has two copies of the recessive allele.

Hatchery Considerations

If you intend to sell or distribute chicks, consider hatchery management, including brooding, vaccination schedules, and customer relationships.

Seek Advice and Resources

Join local or online poultry associations, forums, and social media groups to connect with experienced breeders and access valuable resources and advice.

Expanding Your Flock

Expanding your flock is a rewarding endeavor that requires careful planning and consideration. It allows you to experience the joys of raising more chickens, enjoy additional egg production, or even explore the world of breeding.

Assess Your Goals

Before expanding, define your objectives. Are you interested in increasing egg or meat production, diversifying breeds, or simply enjoying the company of more chickens? Understanding your goals will shape your expansion plan.

Coop and Space Preparation

- Ensure your coop and outdoor space are suitable for the new additions.
- Check for adequate ventilation, nesting boxes, roosts, and secure fencing.
- Provide sufficient space for the increased number of birds to roam and forage.

Breed Selection

Consider your goals and preferences when choosing new breeds. Research their suitability for your climate, space, and purposes, whether that is egg-laying, meat production, or ornamental features.

Sourcing New Chickens

You can acquire new chickens through several methods:

- Hatch your own: If you have a rooster, consider hatching eggs from your flock.
- Buy chicks: Purchase day-old chicks from local hatcheries or

breeders.

- Adopt or rescue: if you're not too concerned with the chicken's pedigree or age, consider adopting chickens in need of a home from animal shelters or rescue organizations.
- Trade or barter: Connect with other chicken keepers for potential trades or exchanges.

Quarantine New Birds

As always, quarantine new chickens before introducing them to your existing flock, for at least two weeks. This helps prevent the spread of diseases and ensures the new birds are healthy.

Integration Process

Introduce new chickens to the existing flock gradually. Observe them closely for signs of aggression or bullying. A few common integration techniques include using a "see but do not touch" approach, providing a separate enclosure within the coop, or allowing supervised free-ranging time together.

Nutrition and Care

Ensure all chickens receive the right nutrition. Adjust your feeding plan to accommodate the increased flock size. Monitor their health and address any issues promptly.

Record-Keeping

Maintain records of your expanded flock, including individual bird details, birthdates, and health notes. This will help you track performance, health history, and breeding outcomes.

Egg and Meat Production

- Prepare for increased egg and, potentially, meat production.
- Plan for additional feed, nesting boxes, and egg collection routines.
- Consider what you'll do with the extra roosters.

Flock Dynamics

Continue to monitor and manage the dynamics within your flock. Address behaviors like bullying and pecking and ensure your chickens have adequate space and access to resources.

Managing Broody Hens

If you're expanding through natural hatching, be prepared to manage broody hens, who may become broody while sitting on a clutch of eggs.

Legal and Zoning Regulations

Check local regulations and zoning laws to ensure compliance with any limitations on flock size.

Seek Support and Resources

Connect with local poultry associations and online chicken keeping communities for advice and support when expanding your flock. Share experiences and learn from other keepers.

Review and Adapt

Regularly review your expansion plan and assess whether it aligns with your goals and the well-being of your chickens. Make adjustments as needed.

Conclusion

Ten Important Things to Remember About Chicken Keeping for Healthy, Happy, and Productive Birds

1. Shelter: Provide a secure and well-ventilated coop to protect your chickens from harsh weather conditions.
2. Protection from predators: Implement effective predator-proofing measures such as sturdy fencing, locks, and secure coop design to safeguard your flock.
3. Adequate space: Ensure your chickens have enough space to move, roost, and forage comfortably. Overcrowding can lead to stress, aggression, pest infestations, and health issues.
4. Nutrition: Offer a balanced diet that includes quality chicken feed and access to clean water at all times. The proper nutrition for each stage of life is essential for your flock's overall health.
5. Cleanliness: Maintain a clean coop to prevent diseases, parasites, and pests. Regularly remove waste, replace bedding, and sanitize water and feed containers.
6. Health monitoring: Keep a close eye on your chickens' health and behavior. Learn to recognize signs of illness and address behavioral and health issues promptly.
7. Social dynamics: Understand the social structure of your flock.

Introducing new chickens can disrupt the pecking order, so do it carefully.

8. Egg collection: Collect eggs daily to ensure they are clean and fresh. Dirty eggs can harbor bacteria, and the longer eggs lay in the nest, the higher the chances of it breaking.

9. Breeding considerations: If you plan to breed chickens, select the right breed and ensure optimal breeding conditions. Avoid breeding closely related birds.

10. Laws, regulations, and rules: Be aware of local regulations, zoning laws, and HOA rules regarding chicken keeping. Comply with any requirements to avoid legal issues.

By remembering these key aspects of chicken keeping, you can create a thriving and content flock that provides you with fresh eggs and the joy of raising these charming birds.

Reflecting on Your Chicken Keeping Journey

As you sit in your backyard, watching your flock of chickens cluck and scratch under the warm sun, you cannot help but reflect on your journey as a first-time chicken keeper. This adventure has been a tapestry woven with feathers, eggs, and invaluable life lessons.

When you first embarked on this journey, you may have known little about chickens beyond the fact that they lay eggs. But the learning curve has been steep and rewarding. You finished learning from this guide, but more importantly, you've learned from the chickens themselves.

One of the most profound lessons has been the importance of responsible care. Chickens depend on you for food, water, shelter, and protection. This responsibility has instilled a daily routine that has become as essential as breathing.

Your backyard has transformed into a microcosm of nature. You've witnessed the changing seasons, the cycle of life, and the resilience of your flock in the face of adversity. It's a powerful reminder of your connection to the natural world.

The daily ritual of collecting fresh eggs never loses its magic. The colors and sizes, the warmth of a freshly laid egg in your hand, and the flavor of a farm-fresh omelet are simple pleasures that bring joy each day.

We hope your chickens have deepened your respect and love for life. Each bird has a personality, a role in the flock, and a unique place in their little world.

In closing, *The Complete Guide to Raising Backyard Chickens* has been a comprehensive journey through the world of chicken keeping. We've covered everything from selecting the right breed and preparing your coop to understanding chicken behavior and addressing common challenges. You've learned how to raise chicks, collect fresh eggs, and even explore the path to sustainable and self-sufficient chicken keeping.

As you reflect on your chicken keeping journey, remember that it is a rewarding and ever-evolving experience. Your newfound knowledge and practical skills will serve you well as you continue caring for your feathered friends. But it does not end here. There is always more to explore, new breeds to discover, and further opportunities to enhance your coop and practices.

We hope this guide has not only equipped you with the expertise to nurture healthy and happy chickens but has also enriched your connection to these remarkable creatures. We encourage you to share your experience, insights, and the joys of chicken keeping with others in your community and beyond.

Next Steps for Chicken Enthusiasts

As you embark on your chicken keeping adventure, we would be grateful if you could take a moment to leave a review and share your thoughts on *The Complete Guide to Raising Backyard Chickens*. Your feedback will help us improve and assist fellow chicken enthusiasts on their own journeys. Thank you for joining us on this feathered path. We wish you and your chickens many years of thriving, clucking, and, most importantly, sharing in the simple pleasures of the backyard coop. Happy chicken keeping!

Glossary

- **Alleles:** Variant forms of a gene that determine specific traits or characteristics in an organism. They occupy the same location on a chromosome and can be dominant or recessive in relation to each other. Alleles contribute to the genetic diversity and individuality of organisms. Alleles can be dominant, recessive, or codominant, influencing the outcome of genetic inheritance.
- **Botulism:** Botulism is a serious and potentially fatal bacterial disease that can affect chickens and other birds. It is caused by the bacterium Clostridium botulinum, which produces a toxin leading to paralysis and muscle weakness.
- **Broiler:** A specific type of chicken raised for the primary purpose of meat production.
- **Brooder:** An enclosure or specialized container used to provide a warm and controlled environment for newly hatched chicks. It is designed to mimic the warmth and protection that a mother hen would naturally provide to her chicks.
- **Broody:** The behavior of a hen that exhibits a strong maternal instinct to sit on a clutch of eggs, often with the intention of incubating and hatching them to raise chicks.
- **Candling:** A process used to inspect the contents of an egg, primarily during incubation, to determine its development and quality. It

involves shining a bright light through the eggshell to reveal the interior, making it possible to assess the embryo's growth, detect defects, and identify whether the egg is fertilized or not.

- **Cloaca:** The reproductive and excretory opening in chickens. They expel waste, including feces and urine, as well as lay eggs and mate through their cloacas.

- **Comb:** The fleshy, crest-like structure located on top of a chicken's head, typically between the eyes. Combs come in various shapes and sizes, depending on the chicken breed.

- **Conformation:** The physical structure, overall body proportions, size, shape, characteristics, and appearance specific to a particular breed. Poultry breeders and enthusiasts assess conformation to identify birds that best represent the breed's standard characteristics.

- **Coop:** A shelter or housing structure designed to house and protect chickens from predators, and provide sleeping accommodation and shelter from the elements.

- **Crop:** An expandable, muscular pouch located at the base of a chicken's throat. It is part of the digestive system and serves as a temporary storage chamber for food. Chickens swallow food, which enters the crop, where it softens and begins the initial stages of digestion. The softened food then gradually moves through the digestive tract for further processing. Chickens can regurgitate food from the crop to feed their young or to aid in digestion.

- **Crossbreed:** See *Hybrid*

- **Diatomaceous earth:** A naturally occurring, fine powder made from the fossilized remains of diatoms, which are tiny aquatic organisms. It is widely used in agriculture and pest control for its unique property of being abrasive to insects but safe for humans and animals.

- **Dust bathing:** A natural and essential behavior exhibited by chickens and other birds. It involves the bird vigorously flapping its wings, scratching, and rolling in dry soil or dust to create a dust cloud that covers its body. The bird then wriggles and rubs itself in the loose material to clean its feathers, remove excess oils, and help control external parasites.

- **Ear lobes:** Fleshy, flat, and colored skin patches found on the sides of a chicken's head, just below the ear openings. They vary in color among chicken breeds.

- **Egg binding:** A condition that occurs when a female bird, is unable to expel an egg from her reproductive tract. It can be caused by various factors, including the size of the egg, internal issues, or physical abnormalities. Egg binding is a critical and potentially life-threatening condition that requires immediate veterinary attention.

- **Hackles**: The feathers located on a chicken's neck and back.

- **Heritage breed:** Also known as a heritage chicken, it refers to traditional and historic breeds of chickens that have been raised for generations and have maintained their genetic characteristics through natural mating and selective breeding. Heritage breeds are valued for their adaptability, hardiness, and cultural significance.

- **Hock:** The joint located in the lower part of a chicken's leg, where the shank meets the lower leg or drumstick.

- **Hybrid:** Often referred to as a crossbreed or hybrid chicken, it is the result of breeding two different purebred chicken breeds to create offspring with specific, desirable traits. These traits may include increased egg production, growth rate, or disease resistance. Hybrid breeds are primarily developed for their efficiency in specific aspects of poultry production, such as meat or egg production.

- **Killing cone:** A device used in poultry processing to humanely and efficiently slaughter chickens and other poultry. It is typically made of metal or plastic and is cone-shaped, with a small opening at the point and a larger opening at the wide end.

- **Layer:** A hen, raised primarily for its ability to produce eggs.
- **Lockdown:** The final phase of egg incubation when, typically three days before the expected hatch date, the incubator's settings are adjusted to provide higher humidity, a stable temperature, and limited intervention to create an ideal environment for successful hatching.
- **Mash:** A type of poultry feed that is typically a mixture of crushed or ground grains, legumes, and various feed ingredients.
- **Non-setter:** A term used to describe a hen that lacks the natural instinct to brood. It does not engage in the behavior of sitting on and incubating a clutch of eggs with the intent of hatching chicks, focusing only on laying eggs.
- **Pipping:** The initial stage of hatching when a developing chick inside the egg breaks through the inner membrane and creates a small hole or crack in the eggshell. This hole allows the chick to access oxygen and initiate the process of hatching.
- **Roost:** A raised, horizontal perch within a chicken coop where chickens perch, rest, and sleep.
- **Run:** An enclosed, outdoor area adjacent to a chicken coop where chickens have access to fresh air, natural sunlight, and space for exercise, foraging, and outdoor activities. It provides chickens with an outdoor environment while keeping them protected from potential predators.
- **Secondaries:** A set of feathers on a chicken's wings. They are the smaller feathers that grow on the ulna or lower wing bone and cover the primary flight feathers. Secondaries play a role in the chicken's ability to control its flight and maneuverability, as well as contributing to the overall wing shape.
- **Shank:** The lower part of a chicken's leg, extending from the hock to the foot. It is often covered in scales or feathers, depending on the breed.

- **Sour crop:** A digestive disorder in chickens characterized by the fermentation of food and an overgrowth of yeast in the crop.
- **Spraddle leg/splayed leg:** A common leg deformity in newly hatched chicks. It occurs when the chick's legs splay outwards to the sides, making it unable to stand or walk properly. This condition can be caused by genetic factors, poor incubation conditions, or slippery surfaces in the brooder.
- **Spurring:** The behavior of roosters using their leg spurs, which are pointed, bony growths on the back of their legs, for various purposes, including self-defense, establishing dominance, and mating.
- **Vent:** See *Cloaca*
- **Vent gleet:** A common poultry health issue characterized by a fungal or yeast infection in a chicken's cloaca.
- **Wattles:** Fleshy, pendulous growths located beneath a chicken's beak on each side of its head. Wattles vary in size and shape among chicken breeds.

About the Author

About Raymond Charles

Born in Hamilton, New Zealand, in 1935, Raymond Charles was the second oldest of four siblings. Their dad, Charlie, had bought a parcel of land in the Waikato in a place called Mako Mako (Mocca Mocca). It was a deal from the Government for having served in World War One.

When he married Flora, they grew their farm and their family. Sadly, their third son Bruce, passed away when he was only nine years old, leaving the three siblings growing up on the farm. They had a lot to do and learn on a farm growing up. Over the years, Raymond has worked on and owned various different bits of land, cultivating them and creating something wonderful, gaining a lifetime of detailed knowledge and memories along the way.

References

Benton, T. (2022, June 9). *The best chicken feed for your flock: A guide to choosing the right feed.* Somerzby. https://www.somerzby.com.au/blog/chicken-feed/

Chartier, J. (2021, December 8). *How to get NPIP certified.* Backyard Poultry. https://backyardpoultry.iamcountryside.com/feed-health/how-to-get-npip-certified

Chicken coop floor options: The best flooring materials for your coop. (2023, September 19). Outpost Buildings. https://outpostbuildings.co.nz/blogs/news/chicken-coop-floor-options-the-best-flooring-materials-for-your-coop

Coccidiosis & your chickens - what you need to know. (2018, March 23). Freedom Ranger Blog. https://www.freedomrangerhatchery.com/blog/coccidiosis-your-chickens-what-you-need-to-know/

Damerow, G., & Luttmann, R. (2018). *Chickens in your backyard, newly revised and updated.* Rodale Books.

The Happy Chicken Coop. (2015a, May 25). *5 Reasons to keep chickens.* https://www.thehappychickencoop.com/5-reasons-to-keep-chickens/

The Happy Chicken Coop. (2015b, June 8). *Best beginner chicken breeds.* https://www.thehappychickencoop.com/best-beginner-chicken-breeds/

The Happy Chicken Coop. (2018, May 25). *Beginner's guide to raising backyard chickens.* https://www.thehappychickencoop.com/raising-chickens/

The Happy Chicken Coop. (2021a, March 11). *Easter Egger: Everything you need to know about this chicken.* https://www.thehappychickencoop.com/easter-egger/

The Happy Chicken Coop. (2021b, March 15). *The Plymouth Rock chicken: All you need to know.* https://www.thehappychickencoop.com/plymouth-rock-chicken/

The Happy Chicken Coop. (2021c, June 15). *Everything you need to know about chicken combs.* https://www.thehappychickencoop.com/chicken-comb/

The Happy Chicken Coop. (2021d, October 22). *The red star chicken: Egg laying, temperament, and broodiness.* https://www.thehappychickencoop.com/red-star-chicken/

The Happy Chicken Coop. (2022a, December 6). *10 Tips for keeping backyard chickens for beginners.* https://www.thehappychickencoop.com/10-tips-for-keeping-backyard-chickens-for-beginners/

The Happy Chicken Coop. (2022b, December 8). *How to raise chickens with no land.* https://www.thehappychickencoop.com/how-to-raise-chickens-with-no-land/

Heinrichs, C. (2016). *The backyard field guide to chickens: Chicken breeds for your home flock.* Voyageur Press.

Henke, J. (2020a, May 31). *Selling farm eggs*. Successful Farming. https://www.agriculture.com/podcast/living-the-country-life-radio/selling-farm-eggs

Henke, J. (2020b, August 3). *Should you wash eggs or not?* Successful Farming. https://www.agriculture.com/podcast/living-the-country-life-radio/should-you-wash-eggs-or-not

Hermes, J. C. (1995). *How to feed your laying and breeding hens*. https://smallfarms.oregonstate.edu/sites/agscid7/files/pnw477.pdf

How to properly store chicken. (2023). Manitoba Chicken Producers. https://manitobachicken.ca/storing-chicken/

Jennifer. (2019, September 5). *What you should not feed your chickens*. Dine a Chook. https://www.dineachook.com.au/blog/what-you-should-not-feed-your-chickens/

Jennifer. (2019, October 11). *Parts of a chicken you need to know*. Dine a Chook. https://www.dineachook.com.au/blog/parts-of-a-chicken-you-need-to-know/

Johnsen, J. (2020, July 24). *Gardening with chickens - Why chickens and gardens just make sense*. blog.Jungseed.com. https://blog.jungseed.com/gardening-with-chickens-and-why-chickens-and-gardens-make-sense/

Lehr, A. (2022, May 7). *5 chicken enrichment toys & ideas*. Grubby Farms. https://grubblyfarms.com/blogs/the-flyer/chicken-enrichment-ideas

Lehr, A. (2023, February 22). *The ultimate guide to buying chicks*. Grubby Farms. https://grubblyfarms.com/blogs/the-flyer/the-ultimate-guide-to-buying-chicks

Lesley, C. (2020a, August 17). *How much space do chickens need: The complete guide.* Chickens and More. https://www.chickensandmore.com/how-much-space-do-chickens-need/

Lesley, C. (2020b, September 20). *Complete leghorn chicken guide: Colors, eggs, facts and more....* Chickens and More. https://www.chickensandmore.com/leghorn-chicken/

McCallum Made. (2017, February 9). *9 rules for hatching eggs - backyard chicken advice.* Chicken Coops and Tractors Australia. https://www.thechickentractor.com.au/9-rules-for-hatching-eggs/

Michigan State University. (2023). *Chicken breed chart to help choose your chicken.* https://www.canr.msu.edu/uploads/234/69325/Chicken_Breed_Chart_to_Help_Choose_Your_Chicken.pdf

Millman, A. (2023). *Chicken breeds ideal for backyard pets and eggs.* HGTV. https://www.hgtv.com/outdoors/landscaping-and-hardscaping/chicken-breeds-ideal-for-backyard-pets-and-eggs-pictures

Nelson, T. (2021, May 23). *Buff Orpington chickens | Everything to know.* The Garden Magazine. https://thegardenmagazine.com/buff-orpington-chickens-everything-to-know/

Oaks, W. (2022, August 25). *How loud and noisy are buff orpington chickens?* Farmpertise. https://farmpertise.com/how-loud-are-buff-orpington-chickens/

Orpington chickens [everything you want to know answered] (2023). Poultry Pages. https://www.poultrypages.com/orpington-chickens/

Ranson, Z. (2019, October 28). *What chickens can and can't eat.* Nature's Best Organic Feeds. https://organicfeeds.com/what-chickens-can-and-cant-eat/

Roeder, M. (2019). *21-day guide to hatching eggs.* Purina Animal Nutrition. https://www.purinamills.com/chicken-feed/education/detail/hatching-eggs-at-home-a-21-day-guide-for-baby-chicks

Sadie. (2023a, March 22). *Is It Better to Buy Chicks or Hens?* Wisconsin Homesteader. https://wisconsinhomesteader.com/is-it-better-to-buy-chicks-or-hens/

Sadie. (2023b, August 14). *How to emotionally raise meat animals.* Wisconsin Homesteader. https://wisconsinhomesteader.com/how-to-emotionally-raise-meat-animals/

Smith, K. (2017). *All the different types of chicken feed explained.* Backyard Chicken Coops. https://www.backyardchickencoops.com.au/blogs/learning-centre/all-the-different-types-of-chicken-feed-explained

Steele, L. (2023). *Choosing chicken breeds for your backyard.* Fresh Eggs Daily. https://www.fresheggsdaily.blog/2018/03/choosing-chicken-breeds.html

Thurmon, A. (2023). *Caring for chickens 101 - A basic beginners guide on keeping chickens.* Azure Farm. https://www.azurefarmlife.com/farm-blog/caring-for-chickens-101

Turning during incubation. (2023). Poultry Performance Plus. https://poultryperformanceplus.com/information-database/incubation/170-turning-during-incubation

Vaughan, B. (2019). *9 Big benefits of keeping chickens as pets.* Woofpurnay Veterinary Hospital. https://www.woofpurnayvet.com.au/benefits-of-keeping-chickens

What to feed your chickens from chicks to egg-laying hens | IFA's blog. (2023). IFA. https://grow.ifa.coop/chickens/what-to-feed-your-chickens-from-chicks-to-hens

Wyzard, B. (2023). *Yes, hens are noisy: Here's what you can do.* The Featherbrain. https://www.thefeatherbrain.com/blog/noisy-chickens

Image References

905513. (2016). *Chicken, ameraucuna, farm.* [Image]. Pixabay. https://pixabay.com/photos/chicken-ameraucuna-farm-animal-1224516/

Alexas_Fotos. (2016). *Faucet, wildpark poing, chicken.* [Image]. Pixabay. https://pixabay.com/photos/faucet-wildpark-poing-chicken-1314967/

Alexas_Fotos. (2019). *Chicken, poultry, free running.* [Image]. Pixabay. https://pixabay.com/photos/chicken-poultry-free-running-4168127/

creisi. (2014). *Chicken coop, chicken, faucet.* [Image]. Pixabay. https://pixabay.com/photos/chicken-coop-chicken-faucet-poultry-245745/

ELG21. (2020). *Roosters, hens, chickens.* [Image]. Pixabay. https://pixabay.com/photos/roosters-hens-chickens-chicken-coop-5599141/

Göllner, A. (2020). *Hen, chicken, feeding.* [Image]. Pixabay. https://pixabay.com/photos/hen-chicken-feeding-poultry-animal-5642953/

Higginbotham, J. E. (2021). *Chicken, rooster, cockerel.* [Image]. Pixabay. https://pixabay.com/photos/chicken-rooster-cockerel-poultry-6244735/

Hughes, K. (2020). *Chicks, chickens, brooder.* [Image]. Pixabay. https://pixabay.com/photos/chicks-chickens-brooder-farm-5147119/

Langthim, M. (2016a). *Cochin, dwarf cookin, chick*. [Image]. Pixabay. https://pixabay.com/photos/cochin-dwarf-cookin-chick-chicken-1415260/

Langthim, M. (2016b). *Wolf, mongolian, feed*. [Image]. Pixabay. https://pixabay.com/photos/wolf-mongolian-feed-prey-predator-1758231/

Lannuzel, L. (2015). *Chicken, bird, orpington*. [Image]. Pixabay. https://pixabay.com/photos/chicken-bird-orpington-1053045/

munzelminka. (2021). Chickens, hens, birds. [Image]. Pixabay. https://pixabay.com/photos/chickens-hens-birds-landfowls-6078279/

Myriams-Fotos. (2017). *Hatching chicks, egg shell break, bill*. [Image]. Pixabay. https://pixabay.com/photos/hatching-chicks-egg-shell-break-bill-2448541/

Ralphs_Fotos. (2018a). *Chicken, hen, poultry*. [Image]. Pixabay. https://pixabay.com/photos/chicken-hen-poultry-rump-3735598/

Ralphs_Fotos. (2018b). *Faucet, rooster head, crow*. [Image]. Pixabay. https://pixabay.com/photos/faucet-rooster-head-crow-poultry-3632298/

Riemer, K. (2015). *Chicken, chicken run, farm yard*. [Image]. Pixabay. https://pixabay.com/photos/chicken-chicken-run-farm-yard-874507/

rubyclement. (2017). *Hen, chicks, chicken*. [Image]. Pixabay. https://pixabay.com/photos/hen-chicks-chicken-poultry-2379722/

tshatzel. (2016). *Rhode island red, chicken, hen*. [Image]. Pixabay. https://pixabay.com/photos/rhode-island-red-chicken-hen-comb-1927352/

u_fsfcui5kui. (2023). *Chickens, incubator, brood*. [Image]. Pixabay. https://pixabay.com/photos/chickens-incubator-brood-poultry-7763394/

VIVIANE6276. (2019). *Birds, rooster, chicken*. [Image]. Pixabay.

Raymond Charles

Made in the USA
Monee, IL
24 September 2024

66524008R00098